TWO MOMS
IN THE RAW

Raw Chocolate Bars (page 256)

TWO MOMS IN THE RAW

simple, clean, irresistible recipes *for* your family's health

SHARI KOOLIK LEIDICH

Photography by Iain Bagwell

A Rux Martin Book
Houghton Mifflin Harcourt
Boston New York 2015

Copyright © 2015 by Shari Koolik Leidich
Photographs copyright © 2015 by Bagwell Enterprises, Inc.

For information about permission to reproduce selections from this book,
write to Permissions, Houghton Mifflin Harcourt Publishing Company,
215 Park Avenue South, New York, New York 10003.

www.hmhco.com

Library of Congress Cataloging-in-Publication Data
Leidich, Shari Koolik.
Two Moms in the Raw : simple, clean, irresistible recipes for your family's health /
Shari Koolik Leidich ; photography by Iain Bagwell.
pages cm
ISBN 978-0-544-25325-4 (hardback) — ISBN 978-0-544-25314-8 (ebook)
1. Quick and easy cooking. 2. Raw foods. 3. Cooking (Natural foods) 4. Raw food
diet—Recipes. 5. Two Moms in the Raw (Firm) I. Title.
TX833.5.L433 2015
641.5'637—dc23
2014036934
ISBN 978-0-544-25325-4

Book design by Alissa Faden

Food styling: Angie Mosier, Toni Brogan
Prop styling: Katelyn Hardwick

Printed in the United States of America
DOC 10 9 8 7 6 5 4 3 2 1

For my husband, Greg, and children,
Sarah, Rachel, and Owen

For my mom, the other "mom"
of Two Moms in the Raw

Garden Jewel Salad (page 154)

Acknowledgments

A cookbook? Are you crazy?

I decided to go for it. Why not? I develop amazing, healthy snacks for my company, Two Moms in the Raw. I feed family and friends great food.

Could I have written this book without any help? Absolutely not! I would like to thank Adeena Sussman, who took a chance on me, which has turned out pretty well for both of us. We are friends and colleagues, and now she is a member of the Two Moms in the Raw team. Have you ever met someone who gives more than you ask? Shows up when needed? Does amazing work in and out of the kitchen? Well, that's Adeena.

I would also like to thank my literary agent, Celeste Fine. You called me while I was on vacation with my family and convinced me that a cookbook was just the right thing for me. I guess you were right. And Rux Martin—you believed in me, and I thank you.

Who has been my biggest fan from the beginning? My mom, Marsha Koolik, another person who always shows up when I need her. I won the lottery when it came to moms. I would also like to thank my dad, Stanley Koolik, who helped put Two Moms in the Raw on the map.

Thank you to my mother-in-law, Cheryl Leidich, for inspiring me in the kitchen. I did not know the joy of cooking until I met you, although I still struggle finding contentment there at times. Thank you, Jim Leidich, for eating what I make with a smile! And thank you to Jenn and Hector Bonilla for your love and support and to Jonathan and Maryann for your passion in life and food.

Thank you, Gary and Tania, for your endless support and encouragement. And to Scott and Souna, for challenging me in the kitchen and always keeping me on task. I love you.

To all of my friends and family: There are so many of you, and I was told to keep this to one page. You know who you are, and I love you!

I would also like to thank Jeremiah Del Tufo, whose spirit lives on in the Two Moms in the Raw Sea Crackers. I hold you in my heart forever.

This cookbook would never have come to pass if it weren't for all the people who love Two Moms in the Raw snacks. Your support keeps us going. And I thank all of my colleagues who keep us moving forward.

Why am I committed to my health and to feeding the world delicious foods that are good for you? My husband, Greg, and children Sarah, Rachel, and Owen: You are my reason for it all.

CONTENTS

Health-Helping Kelp Noodle Salad with Tamarind Dressing (page 136)

INTRODUCTION

It's true, I've got MS. And yeah, it kind of sucks. But life happens when you're looking the other way. I'd always led a relatively healthy life, exercising daily and putting dinner on the table for my family every night. But when everything changed, it did so seemingly overnight. I was a happily married mother of three living the Rocky Mountain lifestyle I loved. I'm not quite sure why—probably because everyone else was doing it—but I decided to get a flu shot. Little did I know it would be the shot heard 'round the world . . . at least my world. Within days, I went from hiking, walking my dogs, nursing my son, and working out to someone who couldn't hold a pen, felt weak on her strongest days, and had trouble focusing on even the smallest tasks and conversations.

"Maybe you're holding your son wrong?" people would ask, naively thinking it might be causing some sort of nerve damage. But soon after, a neurologist confirmed the diagnosis I am still living with today: multiple sclerosis (MS), an autoimmune disorder that made a mockery of my central nervous system, the network of brain and spinal cord functions that ensures the body works the way it's supposed to. Imagine a computer without a chip or a car without a well-maintained engine, and you get the idea.

Suddenly, the mysterious affliction of optic neuritis (inflammation of the optic nerve) that I suffered in my twenties—plus the fact that I always liked to be in bed by 9:00 p.m.—made perfect sense to me. I'd had undiagnosed pre-symptoms of MS for fifteen years, but nobody had caught on to them.

I'm not known for wasting time, so once the diagnosis was confirmed, I did what I always do when a problem arises: Attack it head-on. On the advice of my doctors, I took the conventional course of action, a cocktail of steroids to ease symptoms of the disease. But rather than help, I believe the steroids destroyed my body. I can still feel the sensation of the drugs whipping through me with the force of a tornado, attacking my left side, which has always been weaker, with extra brutality. One morning I found myself in my daughters' room, weeping uncontrollably. How would I take care of my family? How would I take care of myself? How could I recover to the point where I could get myself to the grocery store, my kids' schools, the gym? Things I had taken for granted now seemed so far away. It was then that I realized the standard course of treatment wasn't going to work for me.

I NEEDED A MORE ACTIVE REGIMEN I COULD MANAGE AND CONTROL, and I began searching for a cure, reading every book I could find and seeking out healers who might help me chart a course that traditional medicine was overlooking. I spent countless hours tracking down people who'd written books claiming their MS was cured—only to discover that they were still living in wheelchairs. Discouragement doesn't even come close to describing what I was feeling; defeated was more like it. A wheelchair simply wasn't an option for me.

However, there was one person's story that resonated strongly: Roger McDougall's. He was a regular person like me who believed he could manage his MS by eating a Paleolithic, yeast-free diet. Soon after, I met with an herbalist from Boulder, Brigitte Mars, who recommended a completely raw lifestyle. She believed that cooked foods lost much of their nutritional value in the heating process. That made sense to me.

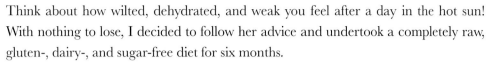

Think about how wilted, dehydrated, and weak you feel after a day in the hot sun! With nothing to lose, I decided to follow her advice and undertook a completely raw, gluten-, dairy-, and sugar-free diet for six months.

Out went the low-carb, high-sugar, fat-free snacks. In came the juicer, the dehydrator, and, most important, the cutting board, where I developed a newfound appreciation for the sound of vegetables being chopped. Very soon, I began to feel better. Stronger. Less tired. Less foggy. Less pain!

In came the juicer, the dehydrator, and, most important, the cutting board, where I developed a newfound appreciation for the sound of vegetables being chopped. Very soon, I began to feel better. Stronger. Less tired. Less foggy. Less pain!

It dawned on me that before my diagnosis, I held very conventional, outdated ideas about what it meant to be a healthy eater. My food plan was designed to keep me thin—but not much else. Sure, I made a dinner salad pretty often and steamed some veggies, but I also took plenty of packaged shortcuts and consumed an ungodly amount of sugar, not giving any of it a second thought as long as I looked halfway decent in my yoga pants.

I may have been in great shape, but my body was depleted of the healthy fuel I needed—and I didn't even know it. Like many American women, by following a low-fat, high-carb plan, I was putting stress on my body and the systems that operate it by depriving it of the tools nature had readily available. I'd been pumping inflammatory foods—particularly processed sugars—into my bloodstream faster than my body could keep up. Excessive consumption of white sugar has been linked to a host of health problems, from obesity and diabetes to hyperactivity in children, joint inflammation, and an increase in illnesses like arthritis. I had to try to reverse the damage if I wanted to not only survive but thrive.

After six months of experimenting with new ways of eating, I was no longer in a health crisis and was ready to reintroduce fruit sugars into my diet, as well as some sweeteners and carbohydrates in limited amounts—mainly so I could prepare food my whole family could enjoy.

The Birth of Two Moms

I REALIZED THAT ONE WAY I COULD KEEP MY DIET HEALTHY AND VARIED WAS by having delicious, raw foods on hand whenever I craved a quick, satisfying bite. I'm a grazer; I love whole meals, but snacking suits my lifestyle and my appetite. In short, I'm always hungry! The snack options in the market, though, didn't hit the spot. The energy bars I tried were dry and gritty, the cereals tasted like animal feed, and the crackers were not worth eating. My husband, Greg, who supported my health quest 100 percent but was skeptical about how good raw snacks could taste, challenged me to create a raw version of the granola he'd just had for breakfast. If it was good enough, he said, he'd eat it. I turned my home into a round-the-clock test kitchen, experimenting with different combinations of fruits, nuts, seeds, and sweeteners in my home dehydrator. I had never seen so many raw almonds in my life!

My raw granola got the GSA (Greg Seal of Approval) a month or so later, and even more important, my kids loved it, finishing every last bite and demanding more. By this time, friends and family were asking for my granola, and I was feeling healthy enough to road test my snacks in the real world. So I packaged up the granola in little cellophane bags and started spreading the (edible) word. At PTA meetings, I popped the trunk to peddle my wares to other moms, some with celiac-suffering or gluten-free kids. Friends showed up at my door to support me and buy a few bags of my products. It was an inspiring experience.

Things were getting very raw and very real. We knew we were on to something, but this was a friendly audience. What would total strangers think? To answer that question, we applied to sell at the highly selective Boulder Farmers' Market. Boulder loves its healthy snacks, and we had a feeling people would be receptive to what we were doing. But though we lived nearby, we had no idea that in high season, tens of thousands of people would be coming through every weekend—many of whom had heard about us through word of mouth.

The response was swift and overwhelming. Once people tasted our samples, they bought us out, sending us back home to burn the midnight oil (well, actually, the dehydrator) to produce enough to supply our stand for the week to come. We were already rocking and rolling when, in 2006, the local Whole Foods asked to test-run our products. They began selling so quickly that Greg left a successful career in telecommunications to officially launch the company with me. My mother, Marsha (the other mom of Two Moms in the Raw), and my dad, Stanley, hopped on the train

14

with us, spreading the word around the country at trade shows large and small. Greg's dad handled the finances. It was all hands on deck—and a family company was born.

NINE YEARS LATER, I CAN'T IMAGINE LIFE WITHOUT TWO MOMS IN THE RAW. Starting this company has brought my family closer together, helped heal me, and inspired me to live, love, and eat differently. The recipes in this book are an extension of everything I have learned over the past decade. What you eat can truly change your life—it certainly did mine.

Don't get me wrong; some days I'm so tired that by the end, all I want to do is crawl into my giant bed, turn up my fan to high to make white noise, and conk out 'til the morning. But don't we all feel that way sometimes? Still, if I'm being honest, those days usually come when I'm not eating the way I know I should, or when I'm not exercising or getting enough sleep, or when I sweat the small stuff.

The majority of the time, though—when I make the right choices and opt to prepare and eat the foods that build me up rather than take me down—I feel like I'm winning the battle. I know that healing is up to me. I'm not going to find the magic-bullet solution in any book, and neither will you. Listen to your own body. Eat the foods that heal you. Cheat occasionally. Exercise daily. Get lots of sleep. And, perhaps most important, laugh a lot (in my case, mostly at myself). That's the path that worked for me. I hope after reading this book, eating my food, and seeing the way I live, you feel the same way.

I like my food simple, sophisticated, and suitable for a quick family meal or a dinner party on the fly. Food is so much more than just something to fill us up; it has the power to heal. Here's to making every bite count—and to making every single one delicious.

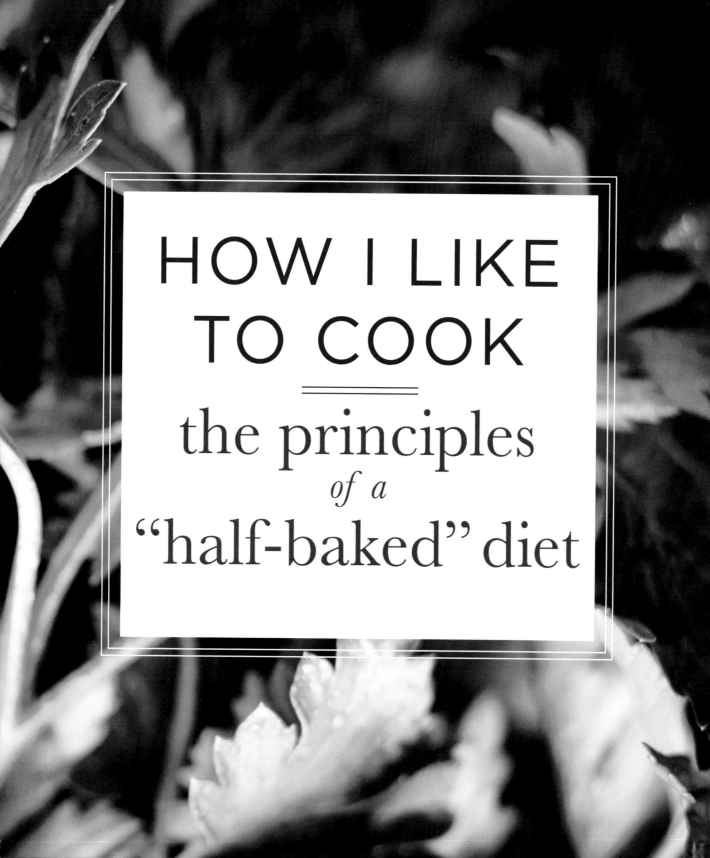

HOW I LIKE TO COOK

the principles
of a
"half-baked" diet

I'm a mom, not a monk, and keeping my kids happy and satis-fied is as important as my health. Though there are many foods I don't eat, there are some I do—always in moderation—that could get me locked up in solitary by the raw police. I believe in occasional "cheating-eating," which contributes to my sanity—and usually reminds me why I changed my diet in the first place.

My goal is always to serve "happens-to" food, by which I mean it tastes amazing and happens to be equally good for you, whether you're looking to lose weight, reduce inflammation, lower blood pressure, or simply have more pep in your step. For me, the ideal recipe is one that's packed with flavor, nutrients, and a healthy twist in the form of vegetable, "grain," spice blend, or condi-ment—and one that can put dinner out as fast as possible. That's because the kitchen is not the place I want to spend every waking moment. I love the smells, tastes, and textures of great food prepared at home, but beyond an hour or so a day, I'd rather be at the gym or walking my dogs in the mountains, working on my growing company, or hanging out with my family.

Some people might feel uncomfortable compelling their families to adopt a whole new way of eating, but not me. Who *wouldn't* want to provide their loved ones with delicious meals and snacks that are lower in sugar, carbohydrates, processed foods, and GMOs (genetically modified organ-isms)? It makes sense to me, and now it makes sense to my friends and family, too. By being the boss of my family's food, I know what goes into every bite—something you can't take for granted in this age of mystery-processing and GMOs. Today my kids request their favorite dishes in this cookbook and my husband has gone vegan. Wonders never cease!

In fact, one of the things that excites me most about my eating and cooking evolution is just how many people I've been able to bring along on my journey to health. I've had friends who have tried every diet under the sun. Most don't continue with these regimens because they feel deprived, hungry, or undernourished. What I now know is that dieting doesn't work, especially when you're eating for health. What does work is a lifelong strategy based on the healthy, natural, largely plant-based foods that our bodies crave, ones that decrease inflammation. By developing a "best of the best" eating plan selected from many other diets—one with principles that make me feel good and allow me to enjoy tasty, life-sustaining foods—I've liberated myself and many friends from feeling guilty about not eating "perfectly." I would love to meet that person who follows one diet to a T and never "cheats." I can do without grains for months at a time, but after a while, I want something more. I also occasionally want something sweet, even though I don't have much of a sweet tooth.

Let's take a few minutes to review some of the diets that have influenced me and my eating habits.

Raw

Raw food is the best food around. I believe this from the bottom of my heart, and though I eat plenty of cooked things, I try to incorporate a raw element into every dish. When I began exploring different ways of eating, I read several books by Gabriel Cousens, MD, a pioneer of the raw-foods movement. Like many others, Dr. Cousens believes that heating food reduces its vitamins and minerals by three quarters, that it literally kills its living nutrients, and that it upsets the delicate balance nature intended for every ingredient. All I know is that since I increased the raw quotient in my diet, I have felt stronger, healthier, more centered, and more powerful physically and emotionally. Raw foods contain more fiber than cooked ones, they're filling, and they allow you to eat less and get more nutrients. What could be bad about that? So adopt my motto: Where There Is Cooked, There Shall Also Be Raw. That means if I make a stir-fry, roast a chicken, or cook up a soup, I'm sure to serve it with a raw side dish as well as a generous topping of fresh herbs. That way I know my family and I will get the nutritional boost only raw foods can provide.

Sugar-Free and Sugar-Less

If I had to attribute my improved health to the elimination of one ingredient, it's refined sugar. Managing MS means keeping the amount of sugar in my blood system low, so one of the first things I did was eliminate white sugar from my diet. In OSL (Old Shari Land), sugar was fine as long as my food was fat-free. Now I know that sugar turns acidic in the body, setting off a whole slew of imbalances (not to mention making me bounce off the walls in ways I prefer to avoid).

Though some diets call for absolutely no sugar, this would only make me and my kids binge out of desperation. Some of the recipes in this book contain small amounts of agave nectar. I use a raw form of agave that has maximum bang for the sweetness buck.

Anti-Inflammatory

I believe that inflammation causes disease. Eliminating it restores balance and health. In *Healing Multiple Sclerosis*, health expert Ann Boroch explains that as MS winds its way through the body, it attacks myelin, sending mixed messages to nerves and causing chronic inflammation. In my case, this impacts everything from motor function and stress levels to the quality of my sleep, the ability to exercise, and the ability to think clearly. Acidic foods are inflammatory, as is refined sugar, which is why I've cut it out altogether. The same goes for refined carbs, which quick-change into glucose in the body—exactly what I'm trying to avoid. I also found that the minute I cut out dairy, which morphs into sugar in the bloodstream, my sinuses cleared up. More important, so did my husband's (read: no more snoring!). I also stopped drinking coffee and consuming most other forms of caffeine, which are highly acidic in nature and can raise blood sugar (I make a "cheating" exception for chocolate, which you'll see in this book). And, for the most part, I've cut out alcohol, too. Every once in a while, a friend brings over a bottle of biodynamic, organic wine, and I have a bit.

Gluten-Free

Originally popularized as a treatment for celiac disease (which causes indigestion, pain, and worse for millions), this diet eliminates all gluten, which can lead to inflammation. The main culprit is wheat, including Kamut—a high-protein strain of wheat—and spelt. Pure oats are gluten-free, but most are contaminated by wheat during growing and processing. Other grains, such as barley and rye, also contain gluten, so I avoid them altogether.

It's important to remember that all gluten-free foods are not created equal. These days, a gluten-free label is far from a guarantee of wholesomeness. More often than not, these foods contain ingredients like refined sugars. I avoid corn and soy, since corn converts to sugar rapidly in the bloodstream. Most soy products are overprocessed, which puts a strain on the colon. Soy also contains a lot of estrogen, which many believe can contribute to early puberty and abnormal development in young girls, something that concerns me as a mom.

Yeast-Free (Anti-Candida)

There is increasing evidence that an abundance of yeast in our system may contribute to illness and disease, from symptoms as simple as indigestion to those as serious as autoimmune disorders. In its natural form, *Candida albicans* (a common yeast) is benign, but many feel that eating certain foods triggers yeast overgrowth in the body, which produces mycotoxins that can compromise health. Many of the foods believed to cause an overpopulation of yeast—refined sugar, carbohydrates, all vinegars except those made from apple cider, alcohol, and dairy—are also no-no's on an anti-inflammatory diet.

Organic

It just seems like common sense to eat food that's as pure as possible in every way, but there's a much more important reason to eat organic: to avoid the crazy amounts of pesticides many farmers use in this country. Unless a food is certified USDA organic, there's no way to guarantee that it has been grown and produced without the harmful synthetic chemicals that can contribute to poor health and encourage disease. According to the Environmental Protection Agency, pesticides are linked to birth defects, nerve damage, cancer, and more. So look for that organic symbol, and shop with it as your guide.

Stress Busters

A newly popular group of natural foods called adaptogens is believed to be a powerful tool in helping us adjust to stress, normalize bodily functions, and achieve mind-body balance. These herbs are thought to support the release of hormones that regulate kidney function and help the body fight stress and disease. Some of them have been part of Indian ayurvedic medicine for more than 5,000 years. Edible adaptogens include dried herbs like eleuthero and ashwagandha, which I sneak into many dishes; tart, crimson goji berries; and aloe vera.

Paleolithic

This high-protein, low-carb eating plan harkens back to the caveman era, and there's a lot to love about it: foods with a low glycemic index, high fiber, less salt, a balanced pH, and plant-based nutrients. It's not revolutionary; it just makes good sense: Eat simply, the way we did before processed foods came into the picture. I like this diet because many of its staples are important to managing the symptoms of my MS. Think nuts and seeds, healthy oils, tons of produce, and high-quality, sustainably raised proteins. That's right, I eat meat! Some believe that animal protein isn't good for people with MS, but through trial and error, I've found that I need it to power me through the day—and get me through the workouts that feed my soul as much as my body. (For more on why I eat meat, see page 184.) A Paleo diet is great for me because it eliminates inflammatory foods like sugar and carbs, but I have to be careful not to overdo the meat, which research shows our bodies never fully digest the way they do plant-based foods.

Plant-Based

If there's one thing we can all agree on, it's that a plant-based diet is a good idea. There's no better way to avoid inflammation, maintain a healthy weight, and keep the health gods in our corner than to eat a diet based on delicious vegetables. No other foods contain as many nutrients, provide the rainbow of colors that makes meals visually appealing, and allow for the kind of variety that keeps things interesting in the kitchen.

Healthy, Healing Foods

Anything that makes it into my kitchen these days is a conscious choice. My pantry and refrigerator are a stockpile of healthy tools designed to keep me and my family healthy and happy. That means I have to do my part, seeking out the staples, produce, and other elements I need to make the food I want to eat. This includes take-out containers—I don't cook every night of the week (gasp!), and I'm not ashamed to admit it. But even when I bring dinner in, I look for foods I can feel good about. Sometimes it's a little more expensive; other times I need to hit an extra store to round out a list of ingredients. But there's no price I won't pay for my health, and this seems like a small one when I think about what's at stake. In the following pages, you'll learn about some of my favorite ingredients.

Oils and Fats

Many of my recipes call for oil, and that's no accident. When processed properly, oils add not only a flavor boost but a nutritional one, too. With all of the research coming out about the health benefits of nuts, I've become an especially big fan of nut oils, but there's a whole range of oils I use in cooking and for flavoring food.

COCONUT OIL

Pressed straight from fresh coconuts, coconut oil is the current darling of the healthy kitchen. Since it remains solid in its natural state in a cool kitchen, it's a great substitute for butter or shortening in baked goods, creating tender, flaky pastries with incredible crumb and moisture. When things heat up a little, it melts into an oil-like substance. It's also got a naturally high smoke point—the temperature at which the oil begins to break down—so it's wonderful for sautéing or pan-frying (see Crispy Zucchini Chips, page 235). But since coconut oil contains saturated fat, which has traditionally been linked to heart disease, it has a mixed reputation within the medical community. I've decided that its health benefits—it has yeast-fighting properties, increases "good" cholesterol, and contains the antioxidant vitamin E—outweigh its potential detractions. Plus, it tastes so darn good.

OLIVE OIL

This is the go-to oil in my house, hands down. With great taste and an impressive résumé of health benefits, olive oil is incredibly versatile.

How I Like to Cook

Loaded with antioxidants, it also contains a ton of monounsaturated fatty acids, which improve "good" cholesterol and lower "bad," protecting your heart in the process. I prefer extra-virgin olive oil for its clean, clear taste and purity. And did you know that in order to be labeled "extra-virgin," the oil has to have an extremely low level of acidity? Keep a few olive oils in the house: ones that have strong peppery or grassy flavors for drizzling on veggies or salads, as well as more neutral ones for sautéing or roasting. I've even taken to frying in olive oil (see Flaxy Sweet Potater Tots, page 239), as long as it's kept to a low bubble; once it gets hot and bothered (above about 350°F), it begins to break down and becomes less healthy, releasing the harmful chemicals known as free radicals into your system.

NUT AND SEED OILS (All of these oils should be stored in the refrigerator, as they will turn rancid or stale faster than others.)

Avocado Oil My favorite thing about this natural elixir is its color: Anything this rich and emerald green just *has* to be healthy. Similar in composition to olive oil, avocado oil is cholesterol-free and high in monounsaturated fatty acids. It's also got chlorophyll (which makes it green), lutein (great for eye health), and vitamin E, which is believed to have heart-healthy benefits—and to give you supple skin and hair.

What I Don't Use: Canola Oil

We're a non-GMO (genetically modified organism) home, and almost all canola oil is made from GMO rapeseeds—no wonder it was renamed canola! GMOs are not our friends; they typically include, among other things, potentially harmful herbicides and may cause possible dangerous side effects. It's true that canola does contain heart-healthy monounsaturated fats and has a fairly high smoke point, but the minute the oil hits its smoke point, it deteriorates and releases damaging free radicals into the oil and the food cooked in it.

Hemp Seed Oil This anti-inflammatory oil has a slightly bitter taste, but its health effects are sweet as can be. Just like the seeds it comes from, it contains alpha-linolenic acid (ALA), which is believed to reduce inflammation, in addition to aiding in heart health. I like to use it in salad dressings with a sweet element (see page 151).

Sesame Oil Sesame oil comes in two forms: toasted, which yields an incredibly rich, slightly smoky flavor; and plain (untoasted), which is lighter in color and has a more delicate, natural sesame flavor. One serving contains almost a full day's recommended allowance of vitamin E, as well as a lot of cholesterol-lowering "good fats." It makes an appearance in lots of my recipes, especially those with an Asian twist.

Walnut Oil and Hazelnut Oil Nutty flavor! Omega-3s! Antioxidants! 'Nuff said. I love using walnut oil to gently flavor tender salad leaves, and I also like it for very low-temperature sautéing (try it with thin slices of carrots, squash, or other autumnal veggies).

The Exotics

Though research is still developing around many of the following ingredients, I've been using some of them for years, while others are more recent additions to my repertoire. Most can be found on Amazon and at Whole Foods or can be ordered from Navitas Naturals, which packages and sells superfood basics from around the world.

AÇAI

Harvested from the açai (ah-*sah*-ee) palm and hailing from tropical climates, açai is similar to a berry. Typically sold as frozen concentrate, powder, or juice, it's packed with antioxidants called flavonoids, effective in combating the spread of free radicals. But be careful—since açai is very tart, many açai products are enhanced with sugar and other sweeteners. If you're buying frozen açai smoothie packs, seek out the unsweetened variety.

ASHWAGANDHA

Considered an A-1 stress-busting adaptogen (see page 21), ashwagandha (ash-wa-*gone*-duh) has long been known in India. I use it to regulate my kidneys and as a proactive stress-buster, and it helps me focus when my attention is flagging or I'm having a midafternoon energy lapse. Because it's bitter, I often dissolve it in water, plug my nose, and bottoms-up a glass in the morning. Other times I slip it into recipes, where it goes unnoticed and does the body a lot of good. I prefer Banyan Botanicals organic ashwagandha powder, available on Amazon.

CACAO NIBS

It's rare that something so indulgent can be so good for you, but that's the case with cacao nibs, made from the crackly hearts of shelled cacao beans. Similar in texture to coffee beans but slightly softer, cacao nibs add chocolaty depth to desserts and snacks. Some are deep and toasty, but the ones I use are raw. They're filled with tons of different nutrients—magnesium, fiber, and iron among them—and loaded with antioxidants. So crunch away—and know you're sending free radicals packing with every bite.

CHIA SEEDS

These tiny Latin American beauties come in black and white varieties. They're crunchy and a good source of omega-3s, and I put a teaspoon into recipes wherever I can.

COCONUT AMINOS

Increasingly available at health food stores, this soy-sauce substitute is made from coconut nectar that's been diluted with water, fermented, and seasoned lightly with salt. It's less salty than soy sauce, so when using it in recipes, think of it as similar to a low-sodium soy; even so, you may need to supplement with a bit of extra salt.

COCONUT FLOUR

In the coming years, you'll be seeing more and more recipes using coconut flour, which is essentially unsweetened dried coconut that's been ground. Gluten-free and versatile, it's a great addition to many desserts, where its slightly nutty, rich flavor is best.

DRIED WHITE MULBERRIES

I can't get enough of these golden beauties, which contain fiber, vitamin C (more than 100 percent of the daily allowance in every serving!), other antioxidants—even protein. Best of all, they taste supersweet but are relatively low in sugar, making them a great grab-and-go snack. With a taste somewhere between caramel and fig, these babies are becoming a favorite among my friends and family. Snack on them raw, add them to raw veggies, or throw a few into a smoothie. Rehydrate them in hot water for a softer texture.

ELEUTHERO (Siberian ginseng)

This Chinese stress-buster is believed to have powerful immune-boosting properties. Eleuthero (i-*loo*-throw) has a mildly herbal flavor that virtually disappears when it's used in recipes. I brew it into a tea, sprinkle it on vegetables, even slip it into meatballs. I usually grind my eleuthero in a spice grinder until almost fine, but not powder-like, and sometimes leave it whole where a dried-herb texture is acceptable. I order Nuherbs organic eleuthero root from Amazon. **Note:** People on blood thinners should avoid eleuthero due to potential conflicts with medication.

GOLDENBERRIES

If you've ever had a Cape gooseberry, also known as a ground cherry, then you've had the fresh version of goldenberries. These tart, sunshine-yellow dried fruits are not only eminently snackable, they've got beta carotene—great for vision—and vitamin A, plus fiber and protein. I throw them into salads and add them to a bowl of grain-free cereal or Top-It-Yourself Millet Breakfast Porridge (page 80). Or check out the luscious Goldenberry and Caramelized Onion Chelish (page 106).

GOMASIO

This savory, crunchy condiment is full of goodness. It usually contains some combination of black and white sesame seeds and often seaweed and herbs. I sprinkle it into salads and soups, and I also top stir-fries with a shake or two for added flavor.

HEMP SEEDS

These pale, nutty, omega-3-packed gems are as adaptable as they are delicious. Sprinkle onto salads, mix into cookies and other desserts, or toss into blended drinks. Once you open them, keep them refrigerated, as they contain a dose of healthy—yet fragile—oil.

KAFFIR LIME LEAVES (also called wild lime leaves, makrut lime leaves)

Fragrant and floral, these glossy green leaves come from a tree indigenous to South and Southeast Asia. You'll find them in many Asian and Indian curries and spice blends, like Green Curry in a Hurry (page 168). Though fresh are preferable, the dried ones—available at Asian markets—still bear the signature aroma and flavor.

KELP NOODLES

Made from sea vegetables bound with a natural coagulant called sodium alginate, these low-carb, virtually calorie-free "noodles" have become a staple in my kitchen. They need no heating or cooking, but they can be gently warmed to replace noodles in a stir-fry.

LUCUMA

This Incan superfood, a fruit, is available in the U.S. as a dried powder. Very low on the glycemic index, nutrient-packed lucuma (loo-*koo*-muh) contains micronutrients, including beta carotene, niacin, iron, zinc, and even protein. Its honey-maple flavor makes it a natural for desserts like Frozen Lucuma-Coconut Mousse (page 273) and lightly sweetened dressings like Lemony Lucuma Dressing (page 158). It is also a natural thickening agent.

MAQUI POWDER

Hailing from Chile, antioxidant-rich maqui berries—typically dried and ground into a powder—contain vitamin C and are said to have antiaging properties. With a wealth of antioxidants, this is some powerful stuff. Try it in the Blue-Antioxidant Smoothie (page 58) or sprinkled onto fresh berries.

MESQUITE POWDER

Sweet and nutty, mesquite powder is a superfood that's packed with fiber and low on the glycemic index. It's great in baked desserts and smoothies and as a sweetener and thickener for ice cream.

NETTLES

Also known as stinging nettles, this plant can treat muscle and joint pain, control inflammation, and calm allergies. I often throw them into juices, smoothies, and teas. This under-appreciated miracle plant, which has a mildly nutty, bitter flavor, supports healthy circulation and adrenal health—two very important variables in managing my MS. In warmer months, I cultivate them in my garden in big flowerpots. That way, I can just pop outside, pluck off some buds, and make tea. Don't worry about a little prick—getting a good sting while picking the nettles acts like an antihistamine. (Or you can pick them wearing gloves.) I also dry them when they're abundant and store them in airtight containers so that I can add them to juices and smoothies later.

PSYLLIUM HUSK

This natural, plant-based dietary fiber has become popular in the gluten-free kitchen in recent years. When hydrated, psyllium husk helps bind together dishes that might otherwise require the addition of flour or other sticky ingredients containing gluten. I use this husk to help hold together desserts like Nutty Goji-Millet Crispy Treats (page 266) and savory dishes, including Veggie Burgers (page 163) and Root-tastic Latkes (page 243). A word of caution: Psyllium husk is a powerful binder and can have the same effect on your digestive system. I use this ingredient sparingly in my recipes, and recommend you do the same.

ROSE HIPS

The small berries that remain on rose bushes after the flowers have dropped, rose hips are typically sold dried and last indefinitely if kept in an airtight container. They're loaded with the antioxidants vitamin C and carotenoids and are believed to have anti-inflammatory benefits. I love their mildly fruity, floral, and tart taste, as well as the potent crunch they lend to Superfood Snack Mix (page 248). I also infuse them into a tea essence (page 69)

that you'll want to drink all day. Add them to salads and grain dishes texture, gorgeous color, and—of course—a healthy boost.

YACON SLICES

Imagine a dried apple with superfood power, and you've got yacon. Grown in the Andes, yacon is actually a tuber but has many of the taste attributes of a fruit. Potassium and antioxidants aside, yacon contains a generous dose of natural inulin—not insulin—a subtly sweet starch the body cannot digest that helps regulate glycemic load. Inulin also contains probiotics, which contribute to colon health. I snack on yacon raw, stir it into fruit desserts like Apple and Pear Crumble (page 268), and throw a few slices into a smoothie for subtle sweetness.

ZA'ATAR

Many Middle Eastern nations put their own spin on this tangy spice blend, whose name comes from one of its main ingredients—the hyssop plant. The za'atar you'll most likely find in spice stores or online contains dried sumac, hyssop, oregano, and thyme, plus sesame seeds and salt. Bonus: lots of antioxidants here! I sprinkle it on salads and soups and use it to season chicken (see Za'atar and Lemon Grilled Chicken, page 199) and fish.

Sweeteners

Man cannot live on apple wedges alone: Everyone's got a sweet tooth! I like to give my kids a treat when they want one, so I use a variety of alternative sweeteners—all in moderation.

FRESH FRUIT

If possible, opt for using fresh fruit when sweetening your food. It's nature's candy, and you'd be surprised at how well it does the job, whether it's orange juice in a salad dressing or the pineapple I use in Peanut-Free Thai Noodle Salad (page 140). Though I still try to keep fruit to a minimum, I prefer it to all other natural sweeteners.

COCONUT PALM SUGAR AND COCONUT NECTAR

With a lower glycemic index than cane sugar, golden brown coconut palm sugar, along with its liquid sister, coconut nectar, is my standard for baking and cooking. Don't get me wrong, it's still not a miracle food—its low glycemic index is a matter of debate in the scientific community—but it's a start. It contains far more sucrose than fructose, which is almost universally accepted as a healthier choice since it doesn't increase sugar levels as quickly once it hits the bloodstream. Also, if you stick with an organic, sustainably harvested brand, chances are it's been processed in a more natural fashion than white sugar.

STEVIA

A highly concentrated liquid with 250 times the sweetness of sugar, stevia has come on strong in the past few years. You can't swap it directly for sugar—it's got a distinct aftertaste, and it doesn't have the bulk that cookies and cakes need—but for sweetening liquids like smoothies, shakes, and teas, stevia's the one I turn to again and again. Derived from the plant *Stevia rebaudiana*, stevia can be found in packets, drops, and even baking blends (which I don't recommend, since they usually have additives). Stevia has no nutritional value, but it doesn't spark my craving for sugar as other alternative sweeteners do. I prefer liquid stevia, which is easily dissolved; 3 drops equal 1 teaspoon coconut palm sugar.

MAPLE SYRUP

Maple syrup is a star of the healthy kitchen. Tapped from trees and boiled down to its finished form, maple syrup contains a whole host of vitamins and minerals, including manganese and zinc—plus antioxidant phenolic compounds. I use it in desserts, as an accompaniment to hot Top-It-Yourself Millet Breakfast Porridge (page 80), or drizzled on vegetables before roasting.

How I Like to Cook

MEDJOOL DATES

I love these fudgy, chewy dates as a binder (as in Nutty Goji-Millet Crispy Treats, page 266) or as a sweetener in a smoothie. Dates are filled with fiber, and they've also got an adhesive, sticky quality that binds together raw desserts with ease.

RAW AGAVE NECTAR

Made from the same plant used to make tequila, agave is very sweet—a little bit goes a long way—so use it in moderation, as we do in Two Moms in the Raw products. Seek out a brand that uses minimal processing.

CHICORY SWEETENER

Sold most commonly in the United States under the name Just Like Sugar Table Top, this type of chicory-based sweetener has been popular in Europe for years, where it is considered a diabetic-friendly product. Since its main ingredient is chicory fiber (inulin), it is believed to help regulate blood sugar. Some people aren't partial to its aftertaste, but I think it's more about how you use it—it helps Nut-Butter Lace Cookies (page 263) spread beautifully and gives them their signature texture.

ALLIUMS

I use alliums—an antioxidant-rich group of vegetables that includes onions, leeks, shallots, garlic, scallions, and chives—every day in my kitchen. Though they don't necessarily contain tons of vitamins, alliums are rich in a type of sulfides linked to cancer prevention—as well as immune-boosting vitamin C. Of all the alliums, my favorite—and most frequently used—is garlic, whose benefits far outstrip its stinkiness. In addition to proven antimicrobial qualities, garlic contains high doses of allicin, a sulfurous compound that combats cancer-causing free radicals, protects against heart disease, and possibly lowers cholesterol.

TIP Studies have shown that if you let the garlic sit for 15 minutes after mincing or crushing, it further releases the healthy enzymes in the garlic. Whenever possible, keep garlic raw—but it's still superhealthy when cooked.

BRASSICAS AND CRUCIFEROUS VEGETABLES

When it comes to nutritional efficiency, brassicas—also known as cruciferous vegetables—are exceptional. Not only are they vitamin- and mineral-packed, but they contain sulfur-producing compounds that work like scrubbers, removing toxins and generally cleaning up our bodies. This group of vegetables includes broccoli, bok choy, cauliflower, cabbage, Brussels sprouts, kale, tatsoi, and collard greens. I am especially partial to cabbage varieties, including Napa, green, red, and Savoy. Cabbage contains cancer-fighting properties and fiber and adds crunch to any meal.

RHIZOMES

Two of my favorite ingredients—turmeric and ginger—are part of the rhizome family of underground stems. Whenever I want to add bright, sunny, golden color and an anti-inflammatory element to a dish, I grate in some fresh turmeric, which has a slightly bitter taste and subtle notes of musk and citrus. The real deal tastes nothing like its dusty, dried counterpart, though both contain curcumin, an antioxidant that has anti-inflammatory properties and has been a component of Ayurvedic and Chinese medicine for thousands of years. (**Note:** People on blood thinners should avoid turmeric to prevent harmful drug interactions.) Some studies have shown turmeric to help relieve arthritis pain, stomach pain, and swelling. Grate it into stir-fries, sauces, smoothies, curries, juices—even baked goods, like Crunchy Millet, Carrot, and Turmeric Muffins (page 254). A powerful anti-inflammatory compound called 6-gingerol makes fresh ginger a staple in my kitchen; it helps keep my body in balance. Ginger's antinausea properties are well-known. I use it in everything from sautés and desserts to tea infusions, sauces, and Healing Chicken Soup (page 120).

Seeds and Grains

While it's true that protein-packed quinoa and all kinds of rice are gluten-free and much lower than wheat products on the glycemic index, I still avoid them for the most part. At the end of the day, all grains are starches, starches are carbs, and carbs convert into sugar in your body. That said, they're a good way to add variety to dinner for your family, and I bring them to the table occasionally as an accompaniment to a meal. To optimize their nutrition and make some of their nutrients more easily absorbed by the body, I soak these grains overnight—or just for a shorter time in the morning, depending on my schedule—then rinse and follow the recipe. Sometimes I put the cooking instructions for the grain in the recipe; at other times, the recipe calls for precooked grains, which I like to prepare and keep in the fridge.

MILLET

Millet, which has been around since biblical times, is lower on the glycemic index, so I feel comfortable eating it. Magnesium-rich, gluten-free, and pleasingly nutty, millet can be used as a side dish (see Mung Bean Dal with Mustard Greens and Millet, page 180) or as a component in desserts (see Nutty Goji-Millet Crispy Treats, page 266). We also use it in Two Moms in the Raw products.

To soak and cook millet: In a bowl, cover 2 cups millet with cold water, cover the bowl, and refrigerate for 8 to 12 hours. Drain well and transfer to a medium saucepan. Add 4 cups water and ½ teaspoon fine sea salt and bring to a boil. Swirl to release any millet stuck to the bottom of the pan, cover, reduce to a simmer, and cook until most of the liquid is absorbed, 15 to 17 minutes. Remove from the heat and let rest, covered, until the remaining liquid is absorbed, 5 to 7 minutes. Uncover and fluff. This makes 7 cups. The millet will keep for 3 to 4 days refrigerated.

QUINOA

Closely related to beets, quinoa is the only plant-based food with all nine of the essential amino acids found in animal protein, and it also contains fiber. Many people make the mistake of overcooking it, which makes it soggy and waterlogged.

To soak and cook quinoa: Look for prerinsed quinoa, but if you can't find it, place 2 cups quinoa in a large bowl, cover with cold water, and rub with your fingers until the water becomes cloudy. Drain and repeat two

Soaking Nuts and Seeds

I've always eaten a lot of nuts, and for the last nine years, I've seen the benefits of germinating (soaking) them before use. Many companies claim to sprout their ingredients, but most likely they are germinating them, which is a little different. Before you start having visions of that elementary-school science project when you tried to grow a tree out of an avocado pit, don't worry: You're just giving them a nice water bath before rinsing and draining. Germinating (which is not the same as sprouting, in which sprouts actually emerge from seeds, nuts, and grains) increases the nuts' nutrients and paves the way for them to be more easily absorbed into the bloodstream. (It also makes you less bloated, and, well, you can extrapolate what else it helps eliminate: Think beans!)

You don't need any fancy equipment to soak nuts; it's as simple as covering them with cold water in a bowl, then draining after the appropriate amount of time.

NUT/SEED	SOAK TIME (IN HOURS)
Almonds	8–12
Brazil Nuts	3
Cashews	2–4
Flaxseeds	1–2
Hazelnuts	8–12
Hemp Seeds	8–10
Macadamias	2
Mung Beans	8–24
Pecans	6
Pumpkin Seeds	8
Sesame Seeds	8
Sunflower Seeds	8
SEEDS AND "ONCE-IN-A-WHILE" OPTIONS	
Millet	8–12
Quinoa	8–12
Wild Rice	8–12

The nuts and seeds must be dried after soaking, either by dehydrating or baking, to prevent the growth of mold. Dehydrate them at 118°F for 8 to 12 hours, depending on the nut or seed.

To dry them in the oven: Spread in a single layer on parchment-lined baking sheets and bake at 350°F until fragrant and dry, stirring if necessary, 15 to 20 minutes, depending on the nut or seed.

TIP Unfiltered apple cider vinegar has probiotic qualities. Add a tablespoon of vinegar and a generous dash of fine sea salt to your soaking liquid.

more times, until the water runs clear. Then, no matter which type of quinoa you're using, cover the quinoa with cold water, cover, and refrigerate for 8 to 12 hours. Drain the quinoa, transfer it to a saucepan, and cover with 3 inches of water. Bring to a boil, reduce the heat to medium-low, and cook until the grains look plumped and a white, squiggly thread appears on each grain, 12 to 13 minutes. Drain well in a colander, and then—this is important—spread the quinoa in a single, shallow layer on a baking sheet and allow to dry for 30 minutes, fluffing occasionally with a fork. This step removes additional moisture from the quinoa and lets it absorb flavor. If you don't have the time for this, return the quinoa to the saucepan after draining and cook, stirring, over medium heat, until additional moisture evaporates. This makes 6 cups. The quinoa will keep for 3 to 4 days refrigerated.

Nuts and Nut Milk

Nuts are good for you! They're fiber-filled, infused with healthy oils, and fill you up better than most snack foods—that's why they're the first ingredient in our Two Moms in the Raw Nut Bars. Nuts are also rich in omega-3s and other important nutrients and have cholesterol-reducing properties. My favorites are walnuts and almonds. When I eat them, I am less hungry and less jittery and feel as though I've indulged.

A study in the *New England Journal of Medicine* found that after following nearly 120,000 people for decades, those who ate nuts on a regular basis had lower rates of cancer, respiratory problems, and heart disease—and a longer life expectancy. More surprisingly, those who ate a lot of nuts were thinner than the average population. It may seem counterintuitive, but the naturally satisfying combination of fiber, fat, and protein makes nuts a supersensible snacking selection. Most nuts contain the kind of oil that promotes HDL, or "good cholesterol," as well as omega-3s and antioxidant vitamin E. I tend to stick to almonds, walnuts, pecans, and hazelnuts and, in most cases, stay away from cashews (they're surprisingly acidic and inflammatory), and I also avoid pistachios, peanuts, and pine nuts (which are linked to the overpopulation of Candida in the body).

HOW TO MAKE YOUR OWN ALMOND (OR OTHER NUT) MILK

I love creamy almond milk, but many brands contain gums, fillers, and other additives that give them a strange thickness. It's best to make almond milk yourself so you have control over what goes into it. It takes a little time but is surprisingly simple, and the process yields the cleanest, freshest-tasting almond milk you've ever had. Also, some almond milks are now made with toasted nuts, which unnecessarily takes the milk from raw to cooked. I say leave it raw and let the nuts' natural nutrition work for you. Though this recipe calls for almonds, it works well with hazelnuts or walnuts, too.

RAW-MOND MILK

Makes 5 cups

2 cups whole raw, organic almonds, walnuts, or hazelnuts

Cold water for soaking, plus 5½ additional cups water

Dash of fine sea salt (optional)

Sweetener

In a medium bowl, cover the almonds with 2 inches cold water. Refrigerate and soak for 12 hours. Drain, discarding the water. In a high-speed or regular blender, combine the almonds and the 5 cups water and blend on medium speed until pulpy and thick, about 1 minute. Strain the mixture through a nut-milk bag (see page 38) into a bowl or other container, squeezing as much liquid from the pulp as possible. Season with salt, if desired, and sweetener to taste.

Kitchen Gear

Stock your kitchen with these tools and watch your culinary creativity come alive. Five years ago, my equipment arsenal consisted of a couple of dull knives, a cutting board, and a box grater. Now I know better. Having the right gear makes my time in the kitchen infinitely easier and less stressful. When you're dealing with a lot of produce, having the proper tools makes all the difference. None of this equipment is essential—Lord knows I've made a whole meal with a mixing bowl and my bare hands—but it sure makes cooking more fun.

Blender

Every kitchen should come with a high-speed blender, such as one from Vitamix or Blendtec. I don't just use mine every day—I use it multiple times, from making my morning juice (when I don't feel like pulling out my juicer) to making sauces, chopping vegetables, blending dips, pulverizing flaxseeds, and making nut butters. They may be pricey, but boy, are they worth it. Look for refurbished models on manufacturers' web sites. I often use a standard blender as well; you may have to work it a little longer, but it's perfectly fine for most of my recipes.

Dehydrator

I'm particularly attached to this piece of equipment, since it's the appliance that got me started with Two Moms in the Raw. Since most foods are still considered raw when heated under 118°F, I use mine all the time to "bake"—half-bake would be the more exact term—macaroons and bars, dry nuts after soaking, make fruit leather, and much more. I'm partial to the five-tray Excalibur brand, which will run you about $250 on Amazon or Excaliburdehydrator.com and will give you a lifetime of dehydrating pleasure. Special dehydrator-safe drying sheets, bought separately (see below), are used to line the trays and create an easy-to-clean, nonstick environment.

Nonstick Dehydrator Sheets

These easy-release liners cover the dehydrator's racks before you place food on them. They're reusable and can be stored rolled up and secured with a rubber band. To clean them after use, fill a sink with warm, soapy water, submerge the sheets for a few minutes, then wipe with a sponge and rinse clean. I prefer to use the ParaFlexx-brand sheets sold on Amazon and Excaliburde-hydrator.com; other brands can leach plastic or disintegrate more quickly. If you don't have the drying sheets, you can use untreated brown parchment paper as a substitute.

Garlic Press

We practically keep the garlic industry in business in the Leidich household; I can't get enough of it, and it's healthy as all get-out. I occasionally chop by hand, but in most instances, my garlic press does the heavy lifting. Look for a model with a large chamber so you can press more than one clove at a time. Some even come with a little cleaning mold you can use to unclog the press before washing.

Glass Storage Containers

We're a BPA-free house, meaning we avoid plastic wherever possible in favor of other, safer materials. (Bisphenol A, a chemical used in the production of many plastic products, has been linked to some health problems.) There's a cabinet filled with stackable glass containers for storing ingredients, leftovers, cut-up fruits and veggies—you name it. The main challenge: keeping track of those lids, which are like single socks in the laundry—something always mysteriously goes missing. I keep all the lids in a separate storage container and stack them from largest to smallest.

Julienne Peeler

Half the deal with cooking is making it fun for the cook, and a julienne peeler does that. *Julienne* is the French term for "thin strips," and this peeler has serrated teeth that allow you to make long shreds out of things like carrots and cucumbers. Use it in place of a box grater for a pretty flourish with minimal cleanup.

Juicer

I juice whenever I can; some days it's all I'm in the mood for. My juicer is a workhorse, efficiently separating the pulp from the juice in no time. Models labeled "extractor" tend to separate more efficiently, reducing waste and extracting the maximum amount of juice. You can also find cold-press juicers, which release juice without any additional heat. Look for a model that's easy to clean (dishwasher-safe for the metal parts) and can handle everything from greens to pomegranate seeds with ease. Pricey isn't always best; ask around among your friends to see which models they like best. And buy a juicer from a store that accepts returns; sometimes they're lemons straight out of the box. Look for one with a great warranty program or buy it at a store with a generous return policy—again, these babies tend to break! After much testing, I have been impressed with the Jack LaLanne's Power Juicer I purchased at Costco. It's cheap, easy to clean, and extracts the maximum amount of juice from anything I throw its way.

Knives

Since vegetables are at the heart of so much of my cooking, knives are important. Although I often turn to my chef's knife and a paring knife, nothing beats a Santoku—a Japanese invention with oval-shaped grooves above the edge—for chopping veggies. Those grooves prevent the vegetables from sticking to the blade, allowing whatever you're cutting to slide right onto the cutting board. I'm partial to Wüsthof or Henckels models, but dozens of good choices abound.

Microplane Grater

Originally invented by a carpenter's wife from a piece of his professional equipment, this little gadget is indispensable for zesting citrus. I also use it to finely grate the fresh nutmeg, ginger, and turmeric—even garlic—that show up again and again in my recipes. Microplanes come in tons of shapes and sizes; my favorite is the Cuisipro-brand dual grater with different-sized holes on each end. Acquire a collection of different sizes for different purposes.

Nut-Milk Bags

These fine-mesh bags were invented to strain the solids from ground nuts soaked in water to make nut milks (see page 34), but they also work fabulously for juicing with a blender; after you've whirred up your greens or fruits, strain them through the bag for the clearest, cleanest, and freshest juice around.

Parchment Paper

Whenever possible, I avoid plastic wrap in my house. I just don't see the point of exposing my family to any more plastic than necessary. Though a lot of supermarket packaging—not to mention the lids on most glass storage containers—contain plastic, I don't drive myself crazy about this. I just do the best I can. And although there is no concrete evidence regarding health risks of aluminum foil (some believe it accelerates Alzheimer's disease and depletes our environment), just to be safe, I prefer to use organic, unbleached parchment paper for lining baking pans and wrapping food; it gets the job done and encourages browning and crispness just as efficiently as foil.

Salt and Pepper Grinders

I buy pink Himalayan salt or coarse salt and grind it myself; the same goes for whole peppercorns. Using a grinder yields fresher pepper than anything you can buy pre-ground in the store. Just make sure you grind the salt—I've sprinkled large crystals into dressings thinking they would dissolve, and my kids thought they were eating stones. For the sea salt called for in most recipes, use any brand of natural, non-iodized sea salt from the health food store or natural foods section of the supermarket.

My Household Healers

Recipes aside, there are lots of things I do to keep me and my family healthy. You'll always find these natural products in my kitchen or medicine cabinet. I think of them as allies for healthy living.

Fermented Coconut Kefir

Extremely popular these days, kefir—typically made from a dairy base and fermented to encourage the growth of healthy probiotics—also comes in a nondairy, coconut variety. Mildly tangy and tropical, coconut kefir defends intestines against disease-causing bacteria, viruses, and yeast, strengthening the immune system in the process. I am partial to the Inner-eco brand, but try out a few to find your own favorite.

Oregano Oil

When one of the kids feels a sore throat or a cold coming on, this is our first line of defense. Oregano contains powerful antimicrobials that help ward off disease and infection. It's also appreciated for its anti-inflammatory properties, making it a winner in my book.

Shea Butter and Coconut Oil

I use them to soften dry skin on heels, hands, cuticles—you name it. The next time you're cooking with coconut oil, scoop up any small amounts left behind and use them to moisturize your skin and hair.

Homemade Lotion Recipe

Whip this up for the softest skin around. Combine 1 cup shea butter with 1 tablespoon each almond oil and olive oil and ½ teaspoon each lavender essential oil and vitamin E oil.

Tea Tree Oil

Another great antimicrobial, I apply it to my kids' minor cuts and scrapes—and dole it out for teenage pimple eruptions. Don't swallow it, but swirl it around your gums for an added disease-fighting boost.

Traumeel

This homeopathic remedy lists arnica, calendula, and chamomile among its active ingredients and is available as a liquid, a topical gel, an ointment, or pills. It helps ease muscle strains, sprains, and other sports-related inflammations.

CHAPTER 1

juices, smoothies, and other drinks

I love the way it feels to load a bunch of organic, salad-worthy ingredients into the hopper of my juicer and watch the fresh, brightly colored juice stream out. It also makes going to the farmers' market or supermarket extra exciting, since it gives me another avenue for packing plant-based nutrients into my system. Some days when I know I need a boost but feel like staying light on my feet, I'll whip up a juice cocktail that matches my mood or what I think my body needs that day.

While many people meet up with friends for a cup of coffee, I have friends who frequently stop by for a green juice! Since I stick to a largely low-glycemic-load diet, most of my juices rely primarily on vegetables, but I think there's a place for a limited amount of fruit in a juicing regimen—especially when you get the kids involved. Wouldn't you rather have them drinking a pomegranate-grapefruit-strawberry juice than a can of soda? Get them started young on fresh juice, and chances are they'll be less likely to want all that other junk. Ask them what they'd like in their juice and custom make it for them. This chapter also contains other drinks, all with incredible health properties.

While most juices call for a traditional juicer, they can also be made in a high-speed blender, such as a Vitamix. If you choose to juice this way, peel rhizomes like turmeric and ginger, as well as garlic cloves and cucumbers; after blending, strain through a nut-milk bag (see page 38).

the recipes

Mix-and-Match
GREEN POWER JUICE

MY GO-TO JUICE, this is a green machine in a glass. You really can't go wrong as long as you keep the sweet stuff to a minimum and make sure you enhance the drink with anti-inflammatory ginger, garlic, and/or turmeric.

————————*Serves 1 or 2*————————

3 large bunches greens (2 pounds total), such as spinach, dandelion greens, swiss chard, or kale (flat or curly)

Nettles (fresh when in season; when not in season, use dried; see page 27)

2 cups microgreens (avoid bitter varieties like arugula)

Handful of fresh flat-leaf parsley

Handful of fresh cilantro

Handful of fresh mint leaves

1 garlic clove, peeled

1 (1-inch) piece fresh ginger

1 (½-inch) piece fresh turmeric

Small amount of apple or pear (optional)

8 to 10 frozen wheatgrass cubes

Juice all of the ingredients except the wheatgrass cubes. Fill one or two tall glasses with the wheatgrass cubes, add the juice, and serve immediately.

A Word About Wheatgrass

When I walk up to the juicing counter for a wheatgrass shot or juice and I see the wheatgrass sitting there in one of those square plastic mini-planters, I get so nauseated that I want to run in the other direction. Wheatgrass produced in greenhouses contains mold, which is harmful to anyone's diet but is an extra-big no-no for me. Besides, wheatgrass grown under natural sunlight contains more chlorophyll than the greenhouse version. My favorite brand of frozen wheatgrass cubes, Evergreen, is made from fresh, outdoor-grown greens. Opt for those, or ask your juice person where the bar's wheatgrass comes from.

pH-BALANCE JUICE

WHEN I'M CRAVING SOMETHING SWEET, I often have this drink to help support the alkaline in my body and curb my desire for sugar.

———————*Serves 1 or 2* ———————

1 cup fresh grapefruit juice

1 cup fresh watermelon juice

Juice of 1 lemon

Juice of 1 lime

2 tablespoons unfiltered apple cider vinegar

Combine all of the ingredients. Fill one or two tall glasses and serve immediately.

GARDEN-BASKET JUICE

THIS TOMATO-LICIOUS JUICE IS HEALTHIER and fresher than the "I-shoulda-had-a" canned version you can find on supermarket shelves. Filled with vitamin C and potassium, radishes are an underappreciated source of healthy properties, and the beta carotene and superfood boosts I get from the carrots and greens, respectively, can't be beat. About the carrots: It's true, they're relatively high in sugar. And, yes, they're on many a special eater's no-no list. When I first began healing through eating, I cut them out altogether, but I love their taste and color.

———————*Serves 2*———————

1 bunch (6 to 8 ounces) greens, such as beet greens, spinach, Swiss chard, or kale

4 Roma tomatoes

1 bunch nettles (when in season; see page 27)

2 carrots

2 celery stalks

4 handfuls fresh flat-leaf parsley

10 small radishes

Juice all of the ingredients. Pour into two glasses and serve immediately.

Juices, Smoothies, and Other Drinks

INFLAMMATION-BUSTER JUICE

WHENEVER MY NERVES ARE JANGLED or I'm feeling tired, I know that my body must be experiencing inflammation. Whipping up a juice like this is like putting a fire extinguisher to the stressors that throw my body out of whack. If I'm being really careful, I leave out the apple. Sugar is not my friend during those times, which are becoming more rare, thankfully.

———————Serves 1———————

5 celery stalks

1 small apple (optional)

4 ounces sprouts, such as
alfalfa or broccoli

1 small garlic clove, peeled

1 (1-inch) piece fresh ginger

1 (½-inch) piece fresh turmeric

Generous handful of fresh herbs, such
as mint, cilantro, parsley, or basil

Juice all of the ingredients. Pour into a tall glass and serve immediately.

TIP **Think Zinc**
When I see white ridges under my nails, I know my body isn't absorbing zinc. When juiced, leafy greens like spinach release high levels of zinc, which are more easily absorbed into the bloodstream than in their original form.

Fiber and Juice: What's the Story?

Yes, it's true that juicing eliminates some of the "roughage" fiber that can help keep you regular, but if you juice properly, much of the soluble fiber in produce makes its way into your system to provide nutritional benefits. Besides, if you're eating a largely plant-based diet packed with fiber-rich vegetables, you'll get all the roughage you need. I generally try to keep fruits and vegetables separate, since the body digests them differently, but I am not religious about it. I'll add a bit of apple or berry to a veggie drink. It's all about moderation.

FENNEL, CUCUMBER, AND MINT ELIXIR

THIS IS JUICE-AS-SPA-TONIC: THE CELERY, cucumber, and fennel all contain great detoxification properties, and the lime, mint, and ginger feel like ladies-who-lunch touches that take you away for a minute, at any time in the day.

————Serves 1————

1 large English cucumber

1 medium head fennel, stalks trimmed
and discarded (7 ounces after trimming)

2 large celery stalks

1 (1-inch) piece fresh ginger

2 tablespoons fresh mint

½ lime

2 frozen wheatgrass cubes
(see box, page 46)

Juice all of the ingredients except the lime and the wheatgrass cubes. Pour into a tall glass, squeeze the lime juice into the glass, and add the wheatgrass cubes. Serve immediately.

TUMMY-EASE TONIC

WHEN MY STOMACH'S UPSET, I turn to this juice. Cucumber's pH-neutral makeup combined with parsley's detoxifying properties and ginger's stomach-settling benefits right my belly in no time.

————Serves 1————

1 English cucumber

Generous handful of fresh
flat-leaf parsley

1 (1-inch) piece fresh ginger

Juice all of the ingredients. Pour into a tall glass and serve immediately.

my eating day

I recommend front-loading your day with energy, then tapering down as the day goes on. Try to be done eating completely by 7:00 p.m., and you'll be surprised how much better you digest your food and sleep through the night.

8:00 A.M.	Goji Berry, Rose Hip, and Red Clover Tea Essence (page 69). Red clover tea should not be enjoyed later than 4:00 p.m.; although it contains no caffeine, it is a mild stimulant.
9:00 A.M.	Hemp protein shake: 1½ cups almond milk, 3 tablespoons soaked and dehydrated hemp seeds, half an avocado, and 1 teaspoon chlorella powder, an algae rich in chlorophyll and protein.
10:00 A.M.	Mix-and-Match Green Power Juice (page 46).
1:00 P.M.	Half an avocado, scrambled or sunny-side-up egg, drizzle of olive oil, flaky sea salt, freshly ground black pepper.
ANYTIME SNACK	Handful of raw almonds or walnuts or a small piece of Raw Chocolate Bar (page 256) or Two Moms in the Raw Nut Bar.
2:00 P.M.	Bowl of soup, chopped salad.
5:30 P.M.	Peanut-Free Thai Noodle Salad (page 140) with chicken, Coco Loco Macaroons (page 260).

BRUSSELS-APPLE-DANDELION-TURMERIC JUICE

AS A MEMBER OF THE BRASSICA (CRUCIFEROUS) family of vegetables, Brussels sprouts are incredibly beneficial for your health—and rarely thought of for juicing. But the resulting juice is surprisingly tasty.

—————Serves 1—————

1 pound Brussels sprouts

2 cups packed dandelion greens

1 large red apple (or ½ cup apple juice), or less to taste

1 (1-inch) piece fresh turmeric

½ lime

Juice all of the ingredients except the lime. Pour into a tall glass, squeeze the lime juice into the glass, and serve immediately.

Cloth Produce Bags: A Sustainable Way to Extend the Life of Produce

Made of breathable natural fabric, these bags are great for storing produce. Herbs take especially well to the bags, which absorb additional moisture that can make herbs spoil faster. I also keep a bunch of these in my tote bags for the supermarket and farmers' market to cut down on my plastic-bag consumption.

MMMMATCHA AND MINT SMOOTHIE

YOU REALLY CAN'T GET ENOUGH antioxidants in your diet, so I like to find inventive ways to squeeze as many as possible into every eating opportunity. I keep a small can of matcha powder—a very pure form of green tea—in the cupboard for those times when I want to make myself a special treat. Though matcha can be mixed with hot water for a steaming cup of tea, I often use it to make this frothy, icy drink—a Shari-fied version of a minty milkshake. In addition to adding an earthy goodness to the mix, matcha delivers a healthy dose of powerful antioxidants believed to slow aging and boost the immune system.

---Serves 2---

1 cup Raw-mond Milk (page 35) or other unsweetened almond milk

1 cup canned coconut milk

1 teaspoon pure matcha (green tea) powder

10 large fresh mint leaves, plus 2 sprigs for optional garnish

2 tablespoons coconut syrup or 2 to 3 drops stevia sweetener

1 cup ice

Combine all of the ingredients in a blender and blend until smooth. Pour into two tall glasses, garnish each with a mint sprig, if using, and serve immediately, with straws.

BLUE-ANTIOXIDANT SMOOTHIE

EVERYTHING IN HERE IS BLUE, and everything is positively loaded with antioxidant power. The maqui powder also serves as a thickener; if you like a thicker, spoonable smoothie, add a little more. Açai smoothie packs—portion-controlled servings of tart puree—come sweetened and unsweetened and are available in the freezer section at health food stores and supermarkets. Always seek out the unsweetened versions!

————Serves 1————

1 (100-gram) unsweetened frozen açai smoothie pack (see above)

1 cup blackberries

1 cup blueberries

½ teaspoon maqui powder (see page 27), or more to taste

¼ cup cold water, or more as needed

Combine all of the ingredients in a blender and blend until smooth, adding more water to thin if necessary. Pour into a tall glass and serve immediately.

═══════════

KALE, BERRY, AND MAQUI SMOOTHIE

ANTIOXIDANT-RICH AND BERRY-BLUE, TART MAQUI powder adds even more superfood goodness to this smoothie's blueberry blast. The longer this smoothie rests before drinking, the thicker and more pudding-like it becomes.

————Serves 1————

1½ cups blueberries

1 large kale leaf (stalk discarded)

½ teaspoon maqui powder (see page 27)

2 teaspoons coconut palm sugar or nectar (see page 29)

½ cup ice

¼ cup cold water

Combine all of the ingredients in a blender and blend until smooth. Pour into a glass and serve immediately.

CINNAMON-BUN SMOOTHIE

THIS YUMMY, DESSERT-LIKE SHAKE flavored with cinnamon, vanilla, and nuts is incredibly healthy compared with a smoothie weighed down with milk, cream, and conventional sweeteners. If you're buying almond milk instead of making it at home—who can be a superchef every day?—look for brands with minimal gums and fillers; they taste cleaner and let the goodness of the nuts shine through.

————————Serves 1————————

1 cup Raw-mond Milk (page 35) or other unsweetened almond milk

1 cup ice

¼ cup chopped walnuts or pecans, soaked and dehydrated (see page 32)

2 tablespoons raisins

¾ teaspoon pure vanilla extract

1 stevia packet or 3 drops stevia sweetener

¼ teaspoon ground cinnamon, plus more for sprinkling

Combine all of the ingredients in a blender and blend on high speed until smooth. Pour into a glass, sprinkle with cinnamon, and serve immediately.

ORANGE-YOU-GLAD-
YOU-DRANK-THIS?

IN THIS DRINK, ORANGE, IN the form of carrot and turmeric, is the color of health. This is one of the sweeter beverages in my repertoire, but it's a real crowd-pleaser. Daikon gives it a spicy kick, plus the nutritional benefits of vitamin C.

————————Serves 1————————

1 very large or 2 medium carrots

1 (¼-pound) piece daikon radish

1 (1-inch) piece fresh turmeric

1 orange wedge

1 lemon wedge

1 lemon wheel, for garnish

Juice the carrot, radish, and turmeric. Pour into a glass, squeeze the juice of the orange and lemon wedges into the glass, garnish with the lemon wheel, and serve immediately.

Iced Almond
CHAI TEA

SINCE LARGE AMOUNTS OF CAFFEINE aggravate my body's inflammation, I stick to decaffeinated or herbal drinks. In the summertime, this refreshing beverage is a particular favorite for the way it replicates the coffeehouse experience—minus the sugar. Almond milk enhances the taste of the chai, coaxing out the individual spices and adding a pleasingly nutty sweetness you won't get with milk.

———————*Serves 8*———————

8 decaffeinated or herbal chai tea bags

2 cups boiling water

2 cups cold water

4 cups Raw-mond Milk (page 35) or other unsweetened almond milk

Stevia sweetener

Brew the tea bags in the boiling water until you have a very strong tea essence, about 1 hour. Strain the essence into a pitcher, discarding the tea bags. Add the cold water, almond milk, and stevia to taste. Chill until ready to serve. Serve over ice.

OMA'S TONIC

MY MOTHER-IN-LAW, CHERYL, SOMETIMES DRINKS this superhealthy elixir before going to bed. The cranberry juice is great for bladder health, and the aloe vera—which has a neutral, slightly grassy flavor—not only contains essential fatty and amino acids but has stress-busting properties to boot.

————————Serves 1————————

1 (3-ounce) piece aloe vera leaf or
2 tablespoons juiced aloe vera

¼ cup pure unsweetened cranberry
or pomegranate juice

½ large apple or ¼ cup apple juice

Splash of unfiltered apple cider vinegar

¼ cup cold water

Stevia sweetener (optional)

Juice the aloe vera and the apple. Add the juice to a glass with the water, cranberry juice, and vinegar. Sweeten to taste with the stevia, if desired, and serve immediately.

GINGER LIMEADE

YOU'LL NEVER BUY LEMONADE AGAIN after making this kicky lime-and-ginger drink. Juicing and freezing the ginger in individual, portion-controlled cubes makes easy work of whipping up a glass whenever the spirit moves you; the Ginger Juice recipe makes enough for 24 glasses of tonic.

—————————*Serves 1*—————————

2 teaspoons frozen Ginger
Juice (recipe follows)

Juice of ½ lime

1 cup good-quality coconut water,
preferably from a fresh Thai
coconut (see sidebar below)

Stevia sweetener (optional)

Ice, as needed

Seltzer water, as needed

Combine the frozen Ginger Juice with the lime juice, coconut water, and stevia to taste, if using, in a glass. Fill with ice, top off with seltzer water, and serve.

Ginger Juice

—————————*Makes 1 cup*—————————

1 pound fresh ginger

Juice the ginger to yield 1 cup fresh ginger juice. Freeze in 2-teaspoon portions in ice-cube trays. Once they are frozen, pop them out and store, frozen, in a Ziploc bag. Ginger cubes will keep, frozen, for up to 1 year.

Fresh Thai Coconuts

Did you know that fresh coconut water was occasionally used during World War II as a replacement for intravenous saline solution when medical supplies were low? The antioxidant and anti-inflammatory properties in young coconuts are amazing, and the water is also isotonic, meaning it replaces body fluids lost to physical stress or injury. My family chops off the top of fresh coconut and drinks the water. Then we scrape out the tender, snowy meat and eat it straight or add it to Thai dishes. I also recommend Harmless Harvest–brand coconut water, a cold-processed product with incredible flavor.

Juices, Smoothies, and Other Drinks

Goji Berry, Rose Hip, and Red Clover
TEA ESSENCE

CONSIDERED A CANDIDA-KILLER, as well as a source of relief from **PMS** due to the presence of phytoestrogens, red clover tea has a mild, slightly bitter herbal flavor. I start many days with a cup of pure red clover tea; other times I like to include it in this floral, gently herbaceous tea essence, which can be used to flavor ice water to taste for iced tea or hot water for a warming drink. Since red clover is a mild stimulant, make sure you drink this one before 4:00 p.m.

———————*Makes 3 cups*———————

⅓ cup dried goji berries

⅓ cup dried rose hips (see page 28)

1 red clover tea bag

4 cups boiling water

Place the goji berries, rose hips, and tea bag in a medium bowl and cover with the boiling water. Let the mixture sit, stirring gently every 5 to 10 minutes, until cool. Cover and let sit at room temperature for 2 hours. Strain through a fine-mesh strainer into a storage container with a tight-fitting lid, pressing on the solids to release as much flavor as possible. Store for up to 1 week in the refrigerator.

CHAPTER 2

breakfast
dishes

Life's so busy during the week, but weekends are the time for meals you can be proud of if a hungry friend just happens to stop by. My family could eat breakfast all day, so most of these dishes have a versatility that allows them to star at breakfast, lunch, or dinner. Several feature eggs, a convenient form of protein that delivers lutein (a carotenoid) and omega-3s, too. I use only pasture-raised eggs that I know are organic; they're definitely pricey, but their gorgeous, deep-golden yolks and great flavor make them a worthwhile investment.

the recipes

BRUNCHY POACHED EGGS ON SPINACH AND CRESS
with Roasted Red Pepper Sauce

THE LAST THING I WANT to do on a weekend morning is spend hours fussing in the kitchen, so I came up with this gorgeous, nutritious, and awesomely crowd-pleasing meal. Poached eggs provide the protein; once you get the hang of making them, they lose the intimidation factor while still being impressive. (You can use hard-boiled eggs if you don't like runny yolks.) The red pepper sauce practically makes itself, and the bed of greens gets the nutritional job done. Dressing the salad a few minutes before serving wilts the greens slightly. Once you break into those poached yolks and trail them in the piquant sauce, you'll realize you've achieved brunch nirvana.

Serves 4 to 6

For the pepper sauce

1 (16-ounce) jar fire-roasted red peppers, rinsed and drained

2 tablespoons extra-virgin olive oil

Juice of ½ lemon

1 garlic clove, peeled

For the greens

5 cups baby spinach

5 cups watercress

½ cup lightly packed fresh basil, sliced into ribbons

2 tablespoons extra-virgin olive oil

¼ teaspoon fine sea salt

⅛ teaspoon freshly ground black pepper

For the eggs

8 large eggs

1 teaspoon fresh lemon juice or vinegar

Make the pepper sauce: In a blender, puree all of the ingredients until smooth.

Toss the greens: In a large bowl, toss all of the ingredients.

Poach the eggs: Crack the eggs into individual small glass bowls or ramekins. Fill a medium (3- or 4-quart) saucepan one-third full with water and bring to a boil. Add the lemon juice or vinegar. Reduce the heat to a simmer. Using a spoon, swirl the water vigorously in a circular motion to create a vortex. Still swirling, pick up one egg in a bowl, bring the bowl as close to the surface of the water as you can, and slip the egg into the water. Poach the egg until the white is unified and the egg looks like an opaque white blob, 2 to 3 minutes. Using a slotted spoon, carefully remove the egg to a plate, tipping to drain away any excess water. Repeat with the remaining eggs.

To serve, arrange the greens on individual plates, spoon a poached egg on top or alongside, drizzle with the pepper sauce, and serve.

TIP Why watercress? Aside from its peppery bite, it's an antioxidant-rich food that contains vitamin C and as much calcium as milk. It's also got powerful body-detox properties in the form of so-called phytochemicals, which help cleanse the liver and ensure proper organ function.

The Antioxidant Benefits of Dried Spices

Antioxidants come in all shapes and sizes, and there can never be too many of them as far as I'm concerned. If you can't squeeze fresh herbs and spices into your diet on a given day, not to worry: Dried spices pack a wallop of antioxidant power—often as much as fresh. The drying process concentrates the nutritional value, meaning that as little as ½ teaspoon of some dried spices—such as cloves—can contain as many antioxidants as a single serving of fresh fruit or vegetables. The following ten dried spices and herbs are high in antioxidant content. That's why they show up all over my recipes!

Cloves	Thyme	Tarragon
Allspice	Marjoram	Basil
Cinnamon	Saffron	
Rosemary	Oregano	

BEET SHAKSHUKA

I KEEP THE WAY I EAT interesting by swapping in a variety of produce whenever possible. If that means using a veggie that contains a little more sugar—in this case, fiber-filled beets with their beta-carotene-packed leaves—I'm fine with it as long as it keeps me harnessing the power of produce at every turn. A dish with roots in Middle Eastern cuisine, shakshuka typically consists of eggs cooked to perfection in a savory tomato sauce. I keep the flavor profile Mediterranean by seasoning the dish with cumin and add a healthy shot of raw at the end in the form of springy scallions and earthy raw beet greens, which contain immune-boosting carotenoids, including lutein, which protects the eyes.

——————Serves 4 to 6——————

2 pounds assorted beets, such as red, yellow, and Chioggia—whatever you have—including the greens

¼ cup extra-virgin olive oil (divided)

3 garlic cloves, thinly sliced

1 large bunch scallions, whites and greens separated, thinly sliced

1 pound vine-ripened tomatoes, diced

1½ teaspoons ground cumin

1 teaspoon fine sea salt

¼ teaspoon freshly ground black pepper

4 to 6 large eggs

Preheat the oven to 400°F.

Separate the tops from the beets and rinse and dry the beets and greens. Thinly slice the beet greens to yield 1½ cups and set aside; reserve the remaining greens for another use. Peel and cut the beets into ½-inch cubes.

In a heavy, ovenproof 10- or 12-inch skillet, heat 2 tablespoons of the oil over medium-high heat. Add the garlic and scallion whites and cook until softened, 1 to 2 minutes. Add 1 cup of the beet greens and cook, stirring, until wilted, 1 to 2 minutes. Add the beets and cook, stirring, until they begin to soften, about 10 minutes. Add the tomatoes, cumin, salt, and pepper and cook until the tomatoes release their liquid and the liquid is mostly reabsorbed, about 10 minutes.

Add the remaining 2 tablespoons oil to the skillet. Using a spoon, create 4 to 6 wells in the beet mixture and crack an egg into each well. Cook for 2 minutes, then transfer to the oven and bake until the egg whites are set, 2 to 3 minutes. Remove from the oven and garnish with the remaining ½ cup beet greens and the scallion greens. Serve straight from the skillet.

Produce-Bin
FRITTATA

I GET A SERIOUS CASE OF PBG—produce-bin guilt—pretty often. It's what happens when you get overzealous at the market, picking up every gorgeous veggie you see, with visions of the sumptuous, colorful meals you'll make in your spare time. Then life gets in the way, and (cue sad movie music) those zucchini, carrots, peppers, and greens haunt you, wilting away day by day. Even with all the juicing I do, there are always leftovers. Frittata to the rescue! Forgiving and flavorful, a frittata is like an omelet with oomph. Once you slice up your fillings, the dish is simple, starting on the stovetop and finishing in a hot oven. Eggs provide the protein the body needs, making this a complete meal in one dish.

—————————*Serves 6 to 8*—————————

12 large eggs

3 cups packed baby spinach coarsely chopped

1 cup mixed chopped fresh herbs, such as dill, parsley, cilantro, and chives

½ cup extra-virgin olive oil (divided)

2½ cups total combination of chopped onions, red onions, shallots, scallions, and/or leeks

5 garlic cloves, minced

3 small zucchini, thinly sliced

1½ cups cherry tomatoes halved (optional)

1 teaspoon fine sea salt

¼ teaspoon freshly ground black pepper

Preheat the oven to 400°F.

In a large bowl, whisk the eggs, then add the spinach and herbs. Heat ¼ cup of the oil in a 10-inch cast-iron or other heavy skillet over medium-high heat. Add the onions and cook, stirring occasionally, until softened and the edges are lightly browned, 10 to 11 minutes. Add the garlic and cook for about 1 minute. Add the zucchini, tomatoes (if using), salt, and pepper and cook, stirring, until the zucchini and tomatoes are slightly wilted, 3 to 4 minutes. Add the remaining ¼ cup oil and stir to incorporate.

Add the egg mixture, stirring to allow the liquid to seep down to the bottom of the skillet. Cook for 3 to 4 minutes. Transfer the skillet to the oven and bake until the frittata is set in the center, 9 to 10 minutes. Remove from the oven, let cool for 5 minutes, then cut into wedges and serve.

TIP Frittata is also great left over, cold, right out of the fridge!

Top-It-Yourself
MILLET BREAKFAST PORRIDGE

HOT CEREAL ON A COLD DAY? Yes, please. Here in Boulder, we get our share of chilly weather, and I stir up this millet-based porridge when I want a rib-sticking breakfast or when the kids request it (which is often). Millet is a protein-packed seed with a much lower glycemic load than oats or wheat, making it a great candidate for porridge. I enrich the cooked millet with almond and coconut milks and infuse it with warm spices. Then comes the fun part: arranging the meal as a do-it-yourself bar with healthy topping options.

————————*Serves 6*————————

For the millet porridge

¾ cup millet, soaked and drained (see page 32)

1¾ cups water

½ teaspoon fine sea salt

1½ cups Raw-mond Milk (page 35) or other unsweetened almond milk, plus more if necessary

1 cup canned coconut milk

⅓ cup coconut palm sugar or nectar (see page 29)

½ teaspoon ground cinnamon

¼ teaspoon ground nutmeg

¼ teaspoon ground cardamom

Pinch of ground cloves

For the toppings bar

Assorted raw soaked and dehydrated nuts and seeds, such as almonds, walnuts, and pepitas (see page 32)

Chopped dates and dried cherries

Fresh berries

Unsweetened shredded coconut

Flax meal

Coconut palm sugar or nectar (see page 29) or maple syrup

Make the millet porridge: Bring the millet, water, and salt to a boil in a medium saucepan. Reduce the heat, cover, and simmer until the millet is just cooked through, 13 to 15 minutes. Remove from the heat and let sit, covered, for 10 to 15 minutes. Uncover and fluff.

Add the almond milk, coconut milk, coconut sugar, cinnamon, nutmeg, cardamom, and cloves. Bring to a boil, reduce the heat to low, and simmer until the millet absorbs most of the liquid and appears porridge-like, 15 to 20 minutes.

Transfer to a serving bowl. Arrange the ingredients for the toppings bar in small bowls or serving dishes. To serve, ladle the porridge into bowls and invite everyone to sprinkle with a variety of toppings.

JUICING CREPES

ALWAYS LOOKING FOR A WAY to wedge greens and herbs into my family's food, I rejiggered traditional crepe batter by adding chard, chives, parsley, cilantro, and basil to the mix. The resulting gorgeously green, lacy-edged crepes are so easy to make and so yummy that you'll hardly realize how healthy—not to mention versatile—they are. For a breakfast-on-the-go, we fill them with whatever raw veggies we can get our hands on, but they're also great paired with Meaty Maitake Mushroom Filling (page 232) or Jerk-Rubbed Salmon (page 192).

——Makes 9 or 10 (6-inch) crepes——

2 large eggs, plus 2 large egg whites

3 large Swiss chard leaves, chopped (1 cup)

¼ cup lightly packed fresh flat-leaf parsley, cilantro, or a combination

10 large fresh basil leaves

2 tablespoons chopped fresh chives or scallion greens

⅔ cup Raw-mond Milk (page 35) or other unsweetened almond milk

3 tablespoons flax meal

1 large garlic clove, peeled

½ teaspoon psyllium husks (see page 28)

¼ teaspoon fine sea salt

¼ teaspoon freshly ground black pepper

2 tablespoons melted coconut oil (see page 23), plus more for frying

Combine all of the ingredients in a blender and blend until smooth.

Heat a crepe pan or nonstick 9-inch skillet over medium-high heat. Using a pastry brush, generously brush the pan with coconut oil. Working quickly and using ¼ to ⅓ cup batter at a time, pour the batter into the pan and swirl until it no longer spreads in the pan. Cook until tiny bubbles begin to appear in the center of the crepe, 1 to 2 minutes.

Using a silicone spatula, gently flip the crepe, being careful not to tear it (it's a little fragile). Cook for about 40 seconds, then slide it onto a plate. Repeat with the remaining batter, adding coconut oil as needed. As the crepes cool, transfer them to a second plate and separate the crepes with parchment paper. Serve with the filling of your choice.

TIP Chew your food! Although it may seem obvious, I wish someone had shared this advice with me when I was a kid trying to keep up with my brothers at the dinner table. Properly chewing food has been linked to improved digestion and is essential for absorbing the maximum amount of nutrients.

dips, relishes, condiments, and spreads

To me, a dip is not just a dip. It's a multipurpose dish that can be used to satisfy urgent hunger pangs, feed the kids after school, line the inside of a sandwich wrap, or impress guests when served with crackers or crudités. That's why you'll always find one in my fridge, ready for scooping up with a No-Carb Paleo Cracker (page 238) or some veggies or for spreading on a Cauliflower Sandwich Wrap or Pizza Crust (with Choice of Toppings) (page 171). Try each sauce and condiment in this chapter once, and a world of kitchen possibilities will open.

the recipes

GUACAMOLE
with Options

I LIKE TO SAY, "An avocado a day keeps the doctor away." And I believe it! I can extol the virtues of this fruit (yes, it's a fruit) nonstop, but here I'll just promote its most delicious delivery method: guacamole. In less than 5 minutes, you can have the ultimate raw snack, filled with "good" fats, potassium, folates, and fiber. I love how versatile guacamole is. With a few tweaks, you can take the flavors in a million directions. I have a bullet-style blender that makes quick work of this guacamole, but you can also hand-chop the ingredients—and you'll have one fewer appliance to wash. Once the guac is blended, add one—or several—of the healthy mix-ins below, if you like.

————Makes 3 cups————

For the guacamole

1 small shallot, peeled

1 garlic clove, peeled

1 cup loosely packed fresh cilantro

2 large, ripe avocados, pitted and peeled

½ medium ripe tomato

1 teaspoon ground cumin

¼ teaspoon fine sea salt,
plus more to taste

⅛ teaspoon freshly ground black
pepper, plus more to taste

Juice of 1 lime, plus more to taste

For the healthy mix-ins (optional)

½ cup chopped tomato

2 tablespoons pepitas, soaked
and dehydrated (see page 32)

2 tablespoons hemp seeds

2 tablespoons pomegranate seeds

¼ cup finely chopped pineapple
or mango, plus 1 tablespoon
seeded, minced jalapeño

Make the guacamole: In a food processor, a narrow-bottomed blender, or a bullet-style blender, pulse the shallot and garlic until finely chopped. Add the cilantro and pulse until finely chopped. Add the avocados, tomato, cumin, salt, pepper and lime juice and pulse until creamy but not totally smooth. Season with additional lime juice, salt, and pepper to taste.

Stir in one or more of the healthy mix-ins, if desired. Serve immediately.

Dips, Relishes, Condiments, and Spreads

ROASTED GARLIC, PEPITA, AND CILANTRO PESTO

I LOVE ME SOME GARLIC, but it can't always be raw. I think of roasted garlic as garlic candy—its natural sugars caramelize and the cloves soften into malleable pieces. Here they lend complexity and flavor to a novel pesto that includes tons of raw cilantro—a digestion aid that's also a body-detox staple—and pepitas (hulled pumpkin seeds) that are naturally loaded with healthy omega-3s and zinc. Serve this as a spread on a grilled chicken breast sandwich, as a topper for broiled fish fillets, or, best yet, at the center of a pile of raw vegetables.

—————————Makes 1 cup—————————

1 large garlic head, top ½ inch trimmed off, unpeeled

½ cup extra-virgin olive oil (divided)

Fine sea salt and freshly ground black pepper

1 cup pepitas, soaked and dehydrated (see page 32)

1½ cups loosely packed fresh cilantro

Finely grated zest of 1 lime

¼ cup fresh lime juice

Preheat the oven to 375°F.

Place the garlic in the center of an 8-inch square of parchment paper, drizzle with 1 tablespoon of the oil, and sprinkle liberally with salt and pepper. Seal loosely, place on a baking sheet, and roast until the garlic is softened and slightly caramelized, 35 to 40 minutes. Cool, still covered.

Squeeze the roasted garlic from its skins into a food processor. Add the pepitas, cilantro, lime zest, and juice, and process until almost smooth, scraping down the sides of the bowl as necessary. With the motor running, slowly add the remaining 7 tablespoons oil in a steady stream. Transfer to a bowl and season with additional salt and pepper to taste.

The pesto can be stored in the refrigerator in an airtight container for up to 3 days.

EGGPLANT AND WALNUT DIP

A LOT OF PEOPLE AVOID nightshade vegetables—potatoes, bell peppers, eggplant, and tomatoes—which are believed to contain solanine, a toxic alkaloid compound. In truth, only potatoes develop solanine, while the other vegetables don't. That's good news for me, since I rarely eat potatoes anyway—but I love eggplant! This dip captures the eggplant's creamy side—which develops during roasting—and the smokiness it takes on with high heat. Fresh herbs, a sprinkling of heart-healthy walnuts, and a generous splash of olive oil put this dip firmly in the guilt-free category.

———————Makes 3 cups———————

2 large or 3 medium eggplants (2 pounds)

½ cup walnuts, soaked and dehydrated (see page 32), chopped

¼ cup extra-virgin olive oil

2 tablespoons fresh lemon juice

2 tablespoons chopped fresh flat-leaf parsley

1 tablespoon chopped fresh oregano

2 small garlic cloves, minced (1 teaspoon)

¾ teaspoon fine sea salt

¼ teaspoon freshly ground black pepper

Crudités or No-Carb Paleo Crackers (page 238), for serving

Preheat the oven to 450°F.

On a baking sheet lined with parchment paper, roast the eggplant until the skin is puffy and blackened, 35 to 40 minutes. Remove from the oven, cool for 15 minutes, then split the eggplant and cool until the eggplant is easy to handle.

Scoop out the eggplant flesh, discarding the seeds and skin, coarsely chop it, and transfer to a bowl.

Add the walnuts, olive oil, lemon juice, parsley, oregano, garlic, salt, and pepper. Serve with crudités or No-Carb Paleo Crackers.

FIG AND OLIVE TAPENADE

HEART-HEALTHY, ANTI-INFLAMMATORY OLIVES ARE one of my favorite ingredients. I love the convenience of having a few jars of good-quality organic olives in the pantry at all times. Same goes for the dried figs. This recipe can be increased in multiples, and I'd recommend it, since I usually start scarfing it down the minute I turn off the blender. It makes a great spread on sandwiches and wraps.

——————Makes 1½ cups——————

15 dried Mission figs (about 4½ ounces), coarsely chopped

¾ cup walnuts, soaked and dehydrated (see page 32)

1½ cups pitted green olives

1½ tablespoons chopped shallot

1 tablespoon chopped fresh oregano

1 teaspoon chopped fresh thyme

2 tablespoons coconut nectar (see page 29)

3 to 4 tablespoons extra-virgin olive oil

No-Carb Paleo Crackers (page 238), for serving (optional)

Place the figs and walnuts in a blender or food processor and pulse until chopped, about 15 pulses. Add the olives, shallot, oregano, thyme, olive oil, and coconut nectar, and and pulse until chunky-smooth, 10 to 15 more pulses. Serve with No-Carb Paleo Crackers, if desired. The tapenade will keep, covered in the refrigerator, for 3 to 4 days.

Dips, Relishes, Condiments, and Spreads

NACHO RAW-CHO "CHEESE"

I EAT NO DAIRY—AND I MEAN NONE—but sometimes I miss the textures of milk, cream, and cheese. For a football game, a party, or just kicking around, this uncanny re-creation of nacho cheese hits the spot. When whirred up in a high-speed blender, macadamia nuts become creamy, and a blend of spices creates as close as you can get to nacho-cheese flavor without picking up a bag of processed, artificially flavored, and chemical-packed chips. The nutritional yeast is a Candida no-no, but as I have said, I break the rules once in a while. You can choose to leave it out, but the finished product won't taste quite as cheesy.

———————*Makes 2 cups*———————

2 cups macadamia nuts, soaked and dehydrated (see page 32)

1 red bell pepper, chopped

1¼ cups water

1½ teaspoons fresh lime juice

5 tablespoons nutritional yeast (optional)

2 tablespoons paprika

2 teaspoons fine sea salt

1 teaspoon chipotle chile powder

½ teaspoon chili powder

¼ teaspoon smoked paprika

½ teaspoon garlic powder

½ teaspoon onion powder

Crudités or No-Carb Paleo Crackers (page 238), for serving

In a high-speed blender, pulse the macadamia nuts, bell pepper, water, and lime juice until chopped and well blended, 15 to 20 pulses. Add the remaining ingredients and blend until smooth, about 10 seconds, scraping down the sides of the blender as necessary.

Transfer to a container, cover, and refrigerate for at least 2 hours to give the flavors time to meld. Serve with crudités or No-Carb Paleo Crackers.

Store in an airtight container in the refrigerator for up to 3 days.

Dips, Relishes, Condiments, and Spreads

GREEN-E TAHINI

RICH, SAVORY, LEMONY, AND SATISFYING, this tahini sauce hits the spot every time. The most important thing is to start out with the very best pure tahini paste, preferably one imported from Israel or another Middle Eastern country. Better yet, make your own (see below). Tahini may have a lot of calories, but a little goes a long way.

——————Makes 2½ cups——————

3 tablespoons fresh lemon juice, or more to taste

2 large garlic cloves, peeled

1 teaspoon fine sea salt

¼ teaspoon freshly ground black pepper

1 cup raw tahini, store-bought or homemade (see below), stirred

⅔ cup coarsely chopped fresh flat-leaf parsley (divided)

1 cup water, or more as needed

Combine the lemon juice, garlic, salt, and pepper in a blender or food processor and blend on high until the garlic is finely chopped. Stop the blender, add the tahini and half the parsley, then blend on high, adding the water in a slow stream, until the sauce is smooth and almost doubled in volume, 1 to 2 minutes. Stop the blender, add the remaining parsley, and blend until the parsley is finely chopped but still visible, about 15 seconds, adding more water by the tablespoonful if necessary. Taste and add more lemon juice, if desired.

TIP Raw tahini, or pure sesame paste, can be found in many supermarkets, at specialty and gourmet stores, or online at Kalustyans.com.

Homemade Raw Tahini
——————Makes 2 cups——————

2 cups raw sesame seeds

¾ cup untoasted sesame oil or other neutral-flavored oil

Combine the sesame seeds and oil in a blender or food processor and blend until smooth, 2 to 3 minutes, scraping down the sides as necessary. Tahini can be stored, refrigerated in an airtight container, for up to 1 month; stir before using.

Dips, Relishes, Condiments, and Spreads

Creamy
OLIVE AND ARTICHOKE DIP

SANDWICH SPREAD? DIP? You get to choose! You'll never find me without a few jars of artichoke hearts in the house, and this dip is the number-one reason why. In 5 minutes, you've got an appetizer that tastes so creamy, you'd swear it's really fattening or loaded with yogurt or mayo—or both. Neither could be further from the truth! Add to that the nutritional advantages: Artichokes are near the top of the USDA's list of antioxidant-rich foods, and they also contain fiber, folate, and vitamins C and K. So dip, dip, dip away to your heart's content.

—————————— *Makes 2 cups* ——————————

2 (14-ounce) jars water-packed artichoke hearts, drained

¼ cup water

2 tablespoons extra-virgin olive oil

2 tablespoons fresh lemon juice

3 garlic cloves, peeled

½ teaspoon fine sea salt

¼ teaspoon freshly ground black pepper

½ cup pitted green olives, preferably Castelvetrano variety

1 tablespoon chopped fresh oregano

In a blender, pulse the artichokes, water, oil, lemon juice, garlic, salt, and pepper until chunky-smooth, 10 to 15 pulses. Add the olives and oregano and pulse until slightly smoothed out, 5 to 10 pulses. Store refrigerated in an airtight container for 2 to 3 days.

Dips, Relishes, Condiments, and Spreads

WALNUT, ALMOND, HAZELNUT, OR SUNFLOWER SEED BUTTER

IT'S NO SECRET THAT I'M downright obsessed with walnuts and almonds—if I could have a tree in my backyard, I would. They're packed with omega-3s and protein, and I just love their taste. While many companies are adding omega-3s to their packaged goods or offering them as supplements, it's best to absorb the nutrients straight from the source. I'm always looking for something to spread on an apple or celery sticks for the kids after school, and these rich, smooth butters do the trick. I've provided the basic recipe here, then some options for jazzing it up. Spread the cinnamon version on warm No-Carb Paleo Crackers (page 238), and you'll forget that butter and peanut butter even exist! My kids prefer their nut butters a little sweet, so the optional addition of coconut nectar makes everyone happy.

————Makes 3 cups————

3 cups walnuts, almonds, or sunflower seeds, soaked and dehydrated (see page 32)

¼ teaspoon fine sea salt

Coconut oil (see page 23) or neutral-flavored oil (optional)

Flavor boosters (optional)

Sweet: 1 tablespoon coconut nectar (see page 29) or a few drops of stevia sweetener, plus 1 tablespoon coconut oil and ½ teaspoon pure vanilla extract

Spiced: ½ teaspoon ground cinnamon and ⅛ teaspoon ground nutmeg

Place the nuts or seeds and the salt in a high-speed blender or a food processor and process until the mixture begins to form a ball, 15 to 20 seconds. Stop the motor, scrape down the sides, add one of the flavor boosters, if desired, then process until smooth and pasty, 30 to 45 seconds. If you like, add a drop of oil to facilitate the process.

Nut butter can be stored, refrigerated in an airtight container, for up to 1 week.

Omega-3 Fatty Acids

Oily fish like sardines and salmon contain docosahexaenoic acid (DHA), widely considered to be the omega-3 with the most proven health benefits. Walnuts (and flaxseeds) contain another form of omega-3, alpha-linolenic acid (ALA), which converts into two heart-healthy omega-3s in the body. And ¼ cup of walnuts provides over 100 percent of the daily recommendation for omega-3s. Score!

Dips, Relishes, Condiments, and Spreads

SUNFLOWER SEED–HEMP DIP

REMEMBER MOCK CHOPPED LIVER? The nut- and vegetable-packed dip is baaaack! Thanks to its rich taste and party-pleasing personality, this is one throwback recipe I'm happy to usher into the modern era. For such a tiny seed, the sunflower packs in loads of vitamins and minerals, from vitamins E and B to manganese, copper, and folate. Tahini adds richness and more of the sesame seed's good health properties, including a surprising dose of calcium. The lemon is super-important here; if you store the dip in the fridge, add even more just before serving to further brighten the dip's flavor.

—————Makes 3 cups—————

2½ cups sunflower seeds, soaked and dehydrated (see page 32)

½ cup hemp seeds

½ cup raw tahini, store-bought or homemade (page 95)

½ cup fresh lemon juice, plus more to taste

½ cup coarsely chopped scallions

¼ cup coarsely chopped fresh flat-leaf parsley, plus more for garnish

¼ small red onion (2 ounces), cut into chunks

3 tablespoons coconut aminos (see page 26)

2 garlic cloves, coarsely chopped, plus more to taste

Pinch of fine sea salt, plus more to taste

½ teaspoon cayenne pepper

In a blender, combine all of the ingredients and process until smooth, 15 to 20 seconds. Season with additional lemon juice, garlic, and salt. Transfer to a bowl and garnish with parsley. The dip will keep, refrigerated in an airtight container, for up to 1 week.

Fire-Breathing
WHIPPED GARLIC SPREAD

ESSENTIALLY A VERY GARLICKY MAYONNAISE (known in France as aïoli), this fluffy spread makes me happy every time I use it in wraps or as a simple salad dressing or dollop it on grilled or steamed vegetables. I even scoop a little out and use it as the base for a bright, lemony sauté or stir-fry. Nutritionally, you get the benefit of keeping everything raw—olive oil's incredible nutrients are best enjoyed in their natural state, as are the antioxidant and heart-healthy properties found in garlic. Just make sure you keep mints handy, since crazy-strong garlic breath is unavoidable here.

—————————*Makes 2 cups*—————————

½ cup garlic cloves, peeled
(from 2 large heads)

¼ cup fresh lemon juice

¼ teaspoon fine sea salt

2 cups best-quality extra-virgin olive oil

Combine the garlic, lemon juice, and salt in a high-speed blender and blend until smooth. With the motor running on medium, slowly drizzle in the olive oil. Once all of the oil is drizzled in, cover the opening and raise the motor speed to high. Blend until smooth and emulsified, 5 to 10 seconds. The spread can be stored in the refrigerator for 2 to 3 days.

TIPS For a recipe like this, where the garlic is the star, take the time to peel your own cloves extracted from whole heads rather than purchasing peeled cloves; the garlic will be firmer and fresher.

Tell your spouse or partner to get over the problem with garlic breath. Better yet, tell him or her to join you!

Smoky
RAWMESCO SAUCE

THE RICH, SMOKY SPANISH SAUCE called romesco is traditionally made by roasting a slew of vegetables, then layering in flavors like smoked paprika, deep-fried Marcona almonds, and sherry vinegar. While I do caramelize the onion and briefly cook the garlic, I leave the nuts and the rest of the veggies raw—this touch adds a freshness that I think improves upon the original—and I swap in cider vinegar for that telltale tang. The heart of the dish is the smoked paprika, which transforms this sauce into something special. Spread it on sandwiches or serve it with meat or fish, as a dip for vegetables, or on top of Quinoa and Sweet Potato Fritters (page 176).

—————Makes 2½ cups—————

½ cup plus 2 tablespoons extra-virgin olive oil (divided)

1 medium onion, finely diced

4 garlic cloves, minced

½ teaspoon smoked paprika, plus more to taste

1 red bell pepper, coarsely chopped

2 small Roma or 1 large vine-ripened tomato (5 to 6 ounces), chopped

½ cup whole almonds, soaked and dehydrated (see page 32), coarsely chopped

2 tablespoons water

1½ tablespoons unfiltered apple cider vinegar

¾ teaspoon fine sea salt, plus more to taste

¼ teaspoon freshly ground black pepper, plus more to taste

Heat 2 tablespoons of the oil in a medium skillet over medium heat. Add the onion and cook, stirring, until golden, 9 to 10 minutes. Add the garlic and paprika and cook for about 1 minute.

Transfer to a blender and cool slightly. Add the bell pepper, tomato, almonds, water, vinegar, salt, and pepper and begin blending. Add the remaining ½ cup oil in a steady stream and blend until smooth, adding more water by the tablespoonful to loosen, if necessary. Season with additional salt, pepper, and smoked paprika. The rawmesco keeps, covered and refrigerated, for 3 to 4 days.

RAW CITRUS AND CRANBERRY RELISH

MY RAW VERSION OF A CLASSIC Thanksgiving condiment tames the pucker sourness of fresh cranberries and orange peel with just the right amount of maple syrup and raw, crunchy pecans. It's great as a side dish with the traditional fixings.

——————Makes 2 cups——————

2 cups fresh cranberries

1 large orange, unpeeled, quartered

½ cup pecans, soaked and dehydrated (see page 32)

¼ cup pure maple syrup

1 (1½-inch) piece fresh ginger, peeled and coarsely chopped

Place the cranberries and the orange in a blender or food processor, then add the pecans, maple syrup, and ginger. Pulse on low speed until the relish looks grainy but is not completely smooth, 20 to 25 pulses. The relish will keep, stored in an airtight container in the refrigerator, for 4 to 5 days.

TIP Did You Know?

Out of all berries, only blueberries have more antioxidants than cranberries, which are packed with vitamin C, too.

PARSLEY PERSILLADELICIOUS

PERSILLADE (pronounced pehr-si-*yahd*) is a traditional French condiment that improves the taste of anything it touches (and gets bonus points for packing two of my favorite ingredients, parsley and garlic, into every drizzle). It's a favorite with my kids, who slather it on everything and consider it a treat. The longer you let this stuff sit in the refrigerator, the better it tastes. Raw parsley is so much more than a benign plate decorator; it's loaded with antioxidants and vitamins, especially vitamin K, which is essential for blood and bone health.

————*Makes 1½ cups*————

1 cup extra-virgin olive oil

8 garlic cloves, minced

2 cups finely chopped fresh flat-leaf parsley

¼ teaspoon red pepper flakes

½ teaspoon fine sea salt

¼ teaspoon freshly ground black pepper

Combine all of the ingredients in a bowl. Cover and refrigerate until ready to use. The persillade will keep refrigerated for 4 to 5 days.

Dips, Relishes, Condiments, and Spreads

GRAINY MUSTARD

MUSTARD ALMOST ALWAYS CONTAINS WHITE or wine vinegar, and since I use only unfiltered apple cider vinegar, that can be problematic for me, so discovering just how easy it was to make my own by soaking and blending a duo of brown and yellow mustard seeds with a few other ingredients was a breakthrough. The result really does look like store-bought. Bonus: Mustard seeds contain selenium, an antioxidant, and omega-3s.

—————Makes 1 cup—————

¼ cup yellow mustard seeds

¼ cup brown or black mustard seeds

1 cup unfiltered apple cider vinegar

1 medium shallot, peeled

1 to 2 tablespoons water, or more as needed

Place the mustard seeds in a medium bowl and cover with the vinegar. Cover and refrigerate until the mustard seeds are fully plumped, 24 hours.

Transfer the seeds and vinegar to a blender, add the shallot, and blend, drizzling in water by the tablespoonful, until the mixture resembles store-bought grainy mustard—partly smooth, but with some mustard seeds still intact. The mustard keeps indefinitely, refrigerated in an airtight container.

Dips, Relishes, Condiments, and Spreads

CARROT-GINGER DIPPING SAUCE

YOU KNOW THAT ADDICTIVE ORANGE stuff you get on your salad at Japanese restaurants? Well, here's a recipe to make your own. It takes 5 minutes, is full of yummy fresh stuff, and will stop you from ever ordering it in—or buying it in a bottle—again. You can serve it on any greens or veggies, but it's born to be the crowning glory of Nori Rolls (page 196).

————Makes 2 cups————

2 large or 4 medium unpeeled carrots, chopped

1 (2-inch) piece fresh ginger, peeled

1 (1-inch) piece fresh turmeric, peeled

½ cup organic grapeseed or other neutral-flavored oil

¼ cup water

¼ cup fresh lime juice

3 tablespoons coconut aminos (see page 26)

3 tablespoons coconut palm sugar (see page 29)

1 tablespoon unfiltered apple cider vinegar

¼ teaspoon fine sea salt, or more to taste

Puree all of the ingredients in a blender until very smooth, about 30 seconds. Season with a little more salt and serve. The dipping sauce will keep, refrigerated in an airtight container, for up to 1 week.

GOLDENBERRY AND CARAMELIZED ONION CHELISH

SUPERTANGY GOLDENBERRIES ARE A GREAT snack, but this chelish puts their nutrition to good use in a savory preparation. I call it "chelish" because it falls squarely between a chutney and a relish—and is equally versatile. I'd just as soon serve this as a relish with roast chicken or turkey as I would spread it on a wrap.

————Makes 1¼ cups————

1 cup goldenberries (see page 26)

1½ cups boiling water

3 tablespoons extra-virgin olive oil

2 large onions (1 pound),
very thinly sliced

1 tablespoon pure maple syrup

1 teaspoon ground dried
eleuthero (see page 26)

½ teaspoon fine sea salt,
plus more to taste

¼ teaspoon freshly ground black
pepper, plus more to taste

¼ teaspoon red pepper flakes

Place the goldenberries in a medium bowl, cover with the boiling water, and allow to soften while you caramelize the onions.

In a large skillet, heat the oil over medium-high heat. Add the onions and cook, stirring, until they soften slightly, 5 to 6 minutes. Reduce the heat to low and add the maple syrup, eleuthero, salt, pepper, and red pepper flakes. Cook, stirring, until the onions are very soft and caramelized, 25 to 30 minutes. Add the rehydrated goldenberries and their liquid, bring to a boil, reduce the heat, and simmer until thickened, 10 to 15 minutes. Season with a little more salt and pepper. Cool before serving. The chelish will keep, refrigerated in an airtight container, for up to 1 week.

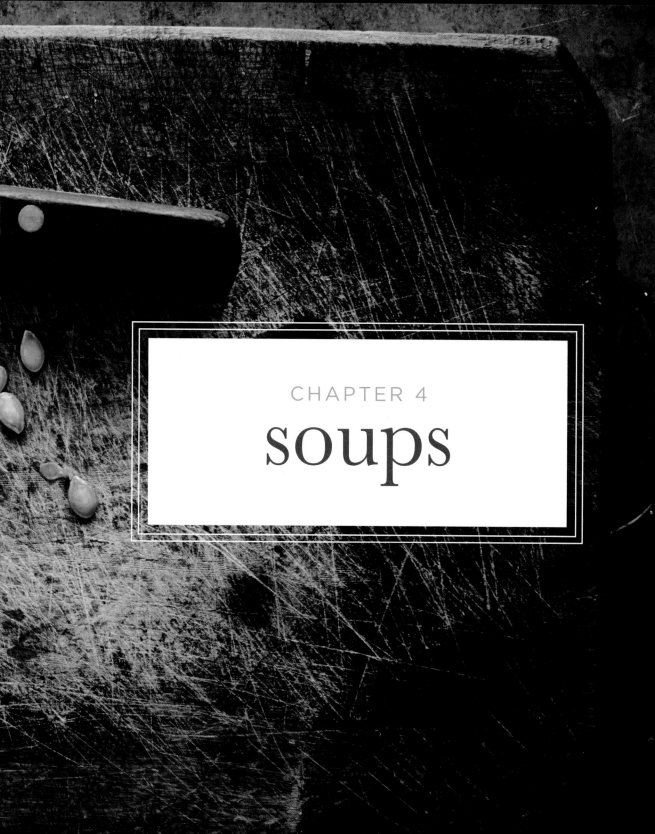

CHAPTER 4

soups

Cold or hot, sweet or savory, soups are swell.

For a busy mom like me, nothing beats the convenience of making a big pot of goodness. Paired with a salad, most of these soups make a full meal, and the kids can ladle up a bowl when they get home from school. The health benefits of soups are nearly unlimited. They're filling, generally contain good stuff, and—research aside—just make a kitchen feel like an extra-warm, cozy place.

the recipes

African Sunbutter Happiness Soup (page 112)

African Sunbutter
HAPPINESS SOUP

HOW MUCH DO WE LOVE this soup in the Leidich household? Let me count the ways: 1) It uses sunflower seed butter as a peanut-free base that tastes incredibly rich and creamy. 2) It gets better as it sits in the fridge, thickening day by day (you can add water or chicken broth to thin). 3) Served with a salad, this soup plays the part of main course like a champ. Make sure to choose a pure sunflower seed butter product, since many are loaded with cane sugar and other sweeteners. (See photo, page 111.)

Serves 6

2 tablespoons extra-virgin olive oil

1 large onion, chopped

1 red or yellow bell pepper, diced

1 large sweet potato, peeled and diced

2 garlic cloves, minced

2 teaspoons finely minced peeled fresh ginger

1 small serrano chili, seeded and diced

2 teaspoons hot smoked paprika

2 teaspoons chopped fresh thyme

2 teaspoons fine sea salt

2 teaspoons chili powder

1 teaspoon curry powder

1 teaspoon ground cumin

2½ cups water, plus more if necessary

1 (28-ounce) can diced tomatoes in juice

¼ cup chopped fresh flat-leaf parsley

1 cup sunflower seed butter, store-bought or homemade (page 97)

¾ cup very finely chopped green kale

Fresh cilantro leaves, for garnish

Sunflower seeds, soaked and dehydrated (see page 32), for garnish

Heat the oil in a 4-quart saucepan over medium-high heat. Add the onion, bell pepper, and sweet potato and cook, stirring, until the onion is tender and the sweet potato begins to soften, 10 to 11 minutes. Add the garlic, ginger, and serrano chili and cook for about 1 minute. Add the paprika, thyme, salt, chili powder, curry powder, and cumin and cook, stirring, for about 1 minute.

A Secret Superfood

They may not be as sexy as goji berries or chia seeds, but humble sunflower seeds get the job done. Loaded with antioxidant vitamin E, they are also believed to be a mood-booster due to their high level of the amino acid phenylalanine, which has been found by some studies to cheer you up.

Add the water, tomatoes and their juice, and parsley, bring to a boil, then reduce the heat and simmer until the sweet potato is very tender, about 15 minutes. Stir in the sunflower seed butter and kale and simmer for 3 minutes.

Remove from the heat and cool slightly, 5 to 10 minutes. Working in batches, puree in a blender or food processor (or use an immersion blender) until smooth, adding additional water as needed to reach the desired consistency. Divide among bowls, garnish with cilantro leaves and sunflower seeds, and serve.

BUTTERNUT SQUASH AND LEMONGRASS SOUP

BUTTERNUT SQUASH IS ONE OF the most versatile ingredients in a smart cook's repertoire, taking on any flavor you throw at it. Here I went with a flavor profile that I love: Thai. Why order greasy takeout when you can get all the same flavors in one healthy, healing bowl? This soup succeeds on lots of levels. It's easy and delicious and contains some of my favorite healthy add-ins: onion, garlic, ginger, and turmeric. I use all fresh herbs, which add so much more intensity than dried. I smash the lemongrass slightly to help release its flavor. Though the soup is typically served hot, no one would judge you if you happened to have it chilled for lunch with a salad.

——————Serves 8——————

1 medium butternut squash, peeled and cubed (about 5 cups)

⅓ cup coconut oil (see page 23) or extra-virgin olive oil (divided)

2 teaspoons fine sea salt (divided)

½ teaspoon freshly ground black pepper (divided)

1 large onion, chopped

5 garlic cloves, chopped

1 tablespoon chopped peeled fresh ginger

2 teaspoons grated peeled fresh turmeric

½ teaspoon red pepper flakes

1 fresh lemongrass stalk, cut into 4 pieces and smashed with the heel of a knife

5 cups water

1 cup chopped fresh chives, plus more for garnish

Preheat the oven to 425°F. Line a baking sheet with parchment paper.

In a large bowl, toss the squash with 3 tablespoons of the oil, 1 teaspoon of the salt, and ¼ teaspoon of the pepper. Transfer to the baking sheet and roast, stirring every 7 to 8 minutes, until the squash begins to soften and its edges are golden, 20 to 25 minutes.

Meanwhile, heat the remaining oil in a large pot over medium-high heat. Add the onion and cook, stirring, until softened and lightly golden, 10 to 11 minutes. Add the garlic, ginger, turmeric, red pepper flakes, and lemongrass and cook until fragrant, about 2 minutes. Add the water and chives, raise the heat, and bring to a boil. Add the roasted squash to the pot, along with the remaining 1 teaspoon salt and the remaining ¼ teaspoon pepper, and return to a boil. Reduce the heat and simmer until the squash is completely soft, 5 to 10 minutes. Remove from the heat, remove and discard the lemongrass, and cool the soup slightly. Working in batches, puree in a blender or food processor until smooth (or use an immersion blender). Divide among bowls, garnish liberally with chives, and serve.

TIP For party presentation, pour into shooter glasses and garnish with chives. Pass as hors d'oeuvres or set out on the table on a pretty tray.

RAWZPACHO

RAW, ROBUST, AND FILLING, GAZPACHO is a a staple of my family's meal plan. You just can't go wrong with a bunch of fresh veggies. To make my gazpacho special, I add crunchy fennel and set up a whole bar of add-ins. That way, everyone can customize his or her own bowl.

———————— *Serves 6* ————————

5 medium vine-ripened tomatoes, coarsely chopped

1 medium English cucumber, peeled, half coarsely chopped and half finely chopped

1 red bell pepper, half coarsely chopped and half finely chopped

1 fennel bulb, half coarsely chopped and half finely chopped

½ small sweet onion, finely chopped

2 garlic gloves, chopped

3 tablespoons fresh lemon or lime juice, or more to taste

3 tablespoons extra-virgin olive oil

1 tablespoon unfiltered apple cider vinegar, or more to taste

1½ teaspoons fine sea salt

½ teaspoon freshly ground black pepper

½ teaspoon celery seeds

¼ teaspoon red pepper flakes

½ cup ice

Extra-virgin olive oil, for drizzling (optional)

For the garnishes

Avocado slices

Chopped radishes

Finely chopped sweet onion

Chopped scallions

Chopped fresh basil, cilantro, mint, and flat-leaf parsley

In a blender or very large food processor, or working in batches, puree the tomatoes, the coarsely chopped cucumbers, the coarsely chopped bell pepper, the coarsely chopped fennel, the onion, garlic, lemon juice, oil, vinegar, salt, pepper, celery seeds, red pepper flakes, and ice until smooth.

Pour into a large bowl or pitcher and add the finely chopped cucumber, finely chopped bell pepper, and finely chopped fennel. Cover and refrigerate for at least 3 hours or overnight.

Season the chilled gazpacho with more lemon juice and/or vinegar. Divide among bowls, drizzle the gazpacho with olive oil, if desired, and serve with the garnishes.

WALNUT, CUCUMBER, AND DILL SOUP

THIS CHILLY, DILLY SOUP TAKES 5 minutes to make, and the walnuts turn it into a one-dish meal. The drizzle of walnut oil on top reinforces the nuts' delicate flavor. If you plan to serve the soup right away, replace half of the water with ice cubes and make sure the cukes are chilled, too.

————Serves 6————

2 cups walnuts, soaked and dehydrated (see page 32), plus chopped walnuts for garnish

2½ cups cold water

2 large cucumbers, peeled and coarsely chopped, plus more for garnish (see Tip below)

¼ cup fresh lemon juice, or more to taste

1½ teaspoons fine sea salt

½ cup chopped fresh dill, plus more finely chopped for garnish

1 tablespoon walnut oil, for drizzling

In a blender or food processor, combine the walnuts with the water and blend on high speed until totally smooth, about 30 seconds. Add the cucumbers, lemon juice, and salt and pulse until almost smooth, 15 to 20 seconds.

Transfer to a bowl, stir in the dill, cover, and refrigerate for 30 minutes to 2 hours.

Season the chilled soup with more lemon juice to taste. Divide among bowls and garnish with the chopped walnuts, cucumber, and dill. Drizzle the soup with walnut oil and serve.

TIP Taste the seeded portion of your cucumbers; if you detect any bitterness, seed the cucumber before chopping.

Healing
CHICKEN SOUP

MY MOM'S CHICKEN SOUP—WHIPPED UP at the first sign of a cold when I was growing up—is the inspiration for this bubbling brew, which I've Shari-ized with some of my go-to food-as-medicine elements. For starters, I brew a pot of eleuthero tea for its perceived anti-inflammatory properties. Then I use a slew of other fresh herbs and spices—garlic, lemongrass, turmeric, and ginger among them—which brings both great taste and health to the pot. The chicken bones add body to the broth.

—————Serves 8 to 10—————

For the tea

3 tablespoons dried (not ground) eleuthero (see page 26)

8 cups boiling water

For the soup

1 (4-ounce) piece fresh ginger, cut into ¼-inch coins

1 (5-inch) piece fresh turmeric, chopped

2 fresh lemongrass stalks, cut into 2-inch pieces and smashed with the heel of a knife

1 whole chicken, cut into 8 pieces

2 tablespoons extra-virgin olive oil

2 medium onions, sliced, or 2 leeks, white parts only, well washed and sliced

10 garlic cloves, peeled and smashed

6 large carrots, peeled and trimmed

5 celery stalks, trimmed

1 turnip, peeled and trimmed

1 rutabaga, peeled and trimmed

1 bunch fresh dill, tied with kitchen twine, plus more for garnish

1 tablespoon fine sea salt, plus more to taste

Make the tea: Using a tea infuser, brew the eleuthero in the boiling water for about 1 hour.

Meanwhile, make the soup: Tie the ginger, turmeric, and lemongrass in a piece of cheesecloth with kitchen twine, leaving a little room for the stuff inside to move around. Set aside.

To an 8- or 10-quart soup pot, add the chicken, cover with 4 inches of cold water, and bring to a boil. Reduce the heat to a vigorous simmer and cook, skimming the scum from the top of the soup as needed, for 15 to 20 minutes.

While the chicken is boiling, heat the oil over medium-high heat in a large skillet. Add the onions and cook, stirring, until just softened, 5 to 6 minutes. Add the garlic and cook, stirring, for 2 minutes. When the broth in the soup pot is clear, transfer the onion mixture to the soup pot, along with the carrots, celery, turnip, and rutabaga. Strain the eleuthero tea directly into the pot, discarding the solids, and then add enough water to almost fill the soup pot to the top.

Bring the soup to a boil. Reduce the heat to a simmer, add the dill bunch, cover, and cook for 1 hour.

Carefully remove the breasts from the chicken to prevent overcooking, leaving the remainder of the chicken in the pot, and reserve in the refrigerator. Continue to cook the soup until the color darkens, 2 to 4 hours (or longer, if desired). During the last hour of cooking, add the salt and the reserved cheesecloth bundle.

Remove and discard the dill bunch and the cheesecloth bundle. Carefully remove the dark-meat chicken and whole vegetables from the soup and cool slightly. Remove the white meat from the refrigerator, then shred the white and dark meat to bite-sized pieces. Discard the bones.

Cut the vegetables into bite-sized pieces. Return the meat to the soup to warm through and season the soup with additional salt to taste. Ladle the soup into bowls and top with a generous sprinkling of fresh dill.

CHAPTER 5

salads

The nerve center of my kitchen is the salad
bowl. Nothing else sees as much activity or gives me as much eating
pleasure. I started out making a lot of salads for my health, but now I
do it because I can't get enough of the crunch, freshness, variety, and
sheer joy of seasonal, organic produce.

Salad is the one thing I am consistently asked to bring whenever I'm
invited somewhere, so I always make sure it's extra good. Once you've
made these salads a few times, run with your own creativity, switching
your favorite raw foods in and out to make them your own.

the recipes

SHARI'S SIGNATURE CHOPPED SALAD
with Herb Dressing

ALL OF THE RAW GREENS I eat are healthy, but the not-so-dirty little secret is that I really just love the way they taste. The crunch, the freshness, the feeling of the garden and the sun all chopped up into tiny pieces never fail to excite me, awaken my palate, and make me feel like I'm being good to my body. This salad has a wealth of great things gathered into one big bowl, and I love it because it's infinitely flexible and customizable. I've done a thousand permutations, using whatever I can dig out of the catacombs of my fridge, schlep in from the greenmarket, or pluck from my own garden. Sometimes I add avocado, sometimes I don't. It's all good. The tart-sweet dressing coats the salad perfectly. If you use hardier vegetables, like broccoli and cauliflower, dress the whole salad. But if the majority of the salad is composed of spinach or other soft, leafy greens and herbs, dress only what you plan to serve on an as-needed basis.

───────── *Serves 8* ─────────

For the herb dressing

1 cup extra-virgin olive oil

6 tablespoons unfiltered apple cider vinegar

¼ cup assorted chopped fresh herbs, such as oregano, dill, parsley, cilantro, and chives

2 tablespoons finely minced shallot

2 large garlic cloves, minced

2 tablespoons coconut nectar (see page 29; optional)

½ teaspoon fine sea salt

¼ teaspoon freshly ground black pepper

For the salad

4 pounds finely chopped assorted vegetables, any of the following: rainbow chard, broccolini or broccoli, cauliflower, dinosaur (lacinato) or curly kale, radicchio, endive, napa cabbage, spinach, microgreens

3 cups minced fresh herbs, such as mint, dill, cilantro, flat-leaf parsley, chives, and chervil

1 cup seeds, such as sunflower seeds or pepitas, soaked and dehydrated (see page 32)

1 English cucumber, unpeeled, very thinly sliced

Make the herb dressing: In a cruet or a jar with a tight-fitting lid, combine all of the ingredients and shake until well combined and slightly emulsified. Or combine all of the ingredients in a blender and blend for 15 seconds.

Make the salad: In a big salad bowl, toss all of the ingredients together except the cucumber slices. Arrange the cucumber slices around the edge of the salad, then drizzle the dressing over the vegetables and serve.

ARTICHOKE AND PERFECT ASPARAGUS SALAD
with Lemony Herbed Vinaigrette

I SOMETIMES MAKE AN EXTRA RECIPE or two of Perfect Asparagus and keep it in the fridge, ready to be snacked upon on its own or tossed into a salad like this one. I'd love asparagus even if it weren't a nutritional star, but the fact that it's got protein (yes, protein), vitamin K, iron, and folate seals the deal. The fennel adds a Paleo-friendly dose of crunch, and marinated artichokes always feel like an indulgence.

Serves 4

For the dressing

⅓ cup extra-virgin olive oil

2 tablespoons fresh lemon juice

1 small shallot, finely minced

1 teaspoon chopped fresh oregano

1 teaspoon chopped fresh thyme

½ teaspoon fine sea salt

¼ teaspoon freshly ground black pepper

For the salad

1 recipe Perfect Asparagus (see below), cut into 2-inch pieces

2 (6-ounce) jars marinated artichoke hearts, drained

1 medium fennel bulb, stalks and tough core discarded, thinly sliced, fronds reserved for garnish

¼ cup thinly sliced fresh basil

½ small red onion, very thinly sliced

Make the dressing: In a large bowl, whisk together all of the ingredients.

Make the salad: Add the asparagus, artichoke hearts, fennel, basil, and red onion to the dressing and toss to coat. Garnish with the fennel fronds and serve.

Perfect Asparagus

Trim 1 pound asparagus and place in a large skillet with ¼ cup water. Bring the water to a boil, cover, steam for 2 minutes, and remove from heat. Remove the asparagus from the skillet and plunge it into an ice water bath to preserve its crispness and color. Drain. The asparagus can be stored in the refrigerator for up to 3 days.

WILD RICE, NUT, AND BERRY SALAD

YOU WON'T SEE ANY OTHER RICE recipe in this book, but wild rice is really a grass, and I love this salad too much to leave it out. When cooked properly, wild rice has an irresistible bite, and the nuts, berries, and scallions are like colorful, nutritious confetti. The vinegar may seem dominant at first, but after about 30 minutes, the flavors mellow. If you're sensitive to the sharp flavor of vinegar or you're serving the salad immediately, add 1 teaspoon less vinegar to the dressing.

Serves 4 to 6

1½ cups wild rice, soaked for 12 hours, rinsed, and drained

2½ cups water

¼ cup extra-virgin olive oil

2 tablespoons unfiltered apple cider vinegar

1 teaspoon Grainy Mustard (page 104)

1 teaspoon fine sea salt

¼ teaspoon freshly ground black pepper

4 scallions, thinly sliced (about 1 cup)

4 breakfast radishes or other radishes, sliced

½ cup almonds, soaked and dehydrated (see page 32), coarsely chopped

½ cup dried white mulberries (see page 26) coarsely chopped

Combine the wild rice and the water in a small saucepan and bring to a boil. Reduce the heat, cover, and simmer until the liquid is absorbed and the rice is firm yet cooked through, 45 to 50 minutes (If necessary, uncover and raise the heat to medium for the last 5 minutes of cooking to evaporate any additional liquid). Remove the rice from the heat and let it rest, covered, for 5 minutes. Fluff with a fork and transfer to a medium bowl.

In a small bowl, whisk together the oil, vinegar, mustard, salt, and pepper. Add to the rice, along with the scallions, radishes, almonds, and mulberries, and toss to combine. If possible, let the salad rest for at least 30 minutes before serving to allow the flavors to blend. Serve cold or at room temperature.

RACHEL'S ISRAELI SALAD

THIS IS THE SALAD YOU SEE piled into a pita sandwich with all the fixings at Middle Eastern restaurants, but I decided to liberate it from all those falafel balls. Since it's my daughter Rachel's favorite, I make a mountain of it so that I can sneak prideful glances as she cracks open the fridge to forage . . . for salad. Some people remove and discard the seeds and jelly-like stuff inside the tomato before chopping, but that's where all the flavor is, so leave it in there! Same goes for the cukes: wash them well to remove any wax, but keep them, and the seeds, intact. The hemp seeds add a boost of protein, omega-3s, and minerals like iron (essential for blood health), magnesium (helps with bone health and blood pressure), and zinc (boosts the immune system).

——————Serves 6——————

5 vine-ripened tomatoes, cored and diced

2 medium cucumbers or 6 small Persian cucumbers, unpeeled, chopped

1 red bell pepper, chopped

1 yellow bell pepper, chopped

½ cup chopped fresh flat-leaf parsley

3 tablespoons hemp seeds

¼ cup fresh lemon juice, plus more to taste

¼ cup extra-virgin olive oil

½ teaspoon fine sea salt

¼ teaspoon freshly ground black pepper

In a large bowl, combine all of the ingredients and toss. Season with more lemon juice. Serve immediately, or refrigerate and allow the flavors to meld for a few hours.

TIP If you don't have lemon juice, swap in lime juice or unfiltered apple cider vinegar. Once this salad sits in the fridge for a few hours, a bunch of liquid accumulates on the bottom of the bowl; it would be a mistake to toss it. Either serve it as a cold broth at the bottom of the salad bowls, or pour it off and store it in the fridge to use as some of the liquid in Rawzpacho (page 116).

WILTED DANDELION GREENS
with Strawberry Vinaigrette

DANDELION GREENS ARE PACKED WITH easily absorbable calcium, iron, antioxidants, and a virtual alphabet of vitamins. But how to tame their pesky bitterness? I've found that wilting them slightly softens the blow, but the real hero here is the raw, vitamin C–and fiber-filled strawberry vinaigrette, which balances out the dandelions' edge and gives you a whole new reason to bring sweet strawberries into the kitchen. If you don't have strawberries, swap in blueberries or raspberries.

Serves 6

For the strawberry vinaigrette

1 small shallot, peeled

¾ cup strawberries, hulled

3 tablespoons extra-virgin olive oil

2 tablespoons unfiltered apple cider vinegar

¼ teaspoon mustard powder

¼ teaspoon fine sea salt

⅛ teaspoon freshly ground black pepper

For the greens

2 tablespoons extra-virgin olive oil or coconut oil (see page 23)

1 large shallot, thinly sliced

2 bunches dandelion greens, well rinsed, dried, and chopped

Fine sea salt and freshly ground black pepper

Make the strawberry vinaigrette: In a blender, pulse all of the dressing ingredients until chunky and incorporated but not smooth and creamy. (If you overprocess, the dressing begins to look like Pepto-Bismol—not good when you're trying to get your kids to eat their greens.)

Wilt the dandelion greens: In a large skillet, heat the oil over medium-high heat. Add the shallot and cook until softened, 1 to 2 minutes. Add the greens and salt and pepper to taste and cook, stirring, until wilted, 2 to 3 minutes. Transfer to a platter, drizzle with the dressing, and serve.

Mango, Avocado, and Kelp
NOODLE SALAD

MADE FROM SEA KELP SPUN like magic into glass-like strands, kelp noodles are a virtually calorie-free food with none of the downsides of pasta, and they have many benefits— namely, the way they take to dressing, herbs, and other produce like a pro. Here, mango, avocado, and crunchy veggies turn this salad into a feast for the senses. Adding cooked salmon or chicken boosts the protein and turns it into a main course.

—————————*Serves 4 to 6*—————————

¼ cup organic safflower oil

3 tablespoons unfiltered apple cider vinegar

1 large garlic clove, minced

¼ teaspoon fine sea salt

¼ teaspoon red pepper flakes, or more to taste

1 (12-ounce) package kelp noodles (see above), such as Sea Tangle brand, rinsed, drained, separated, and fluffed

1 large firm, ripe avocado, pitted and cubed

1 firm, ripe mango, peeled, pitted, and thinly sliced

1 red or yellow bell pepper, finely chopped

¼ small red onion, thinly sliced

¼ cup chopped fresh cilantro

1 sheet nori (seaweed), crumbled

Cooked salmon or chicken (optional)

In a large bowl, whisk together the oil, vinegar, garlic, salt, and red pepper flakes. Add the kelp noodles, avocado, mango, bell pepper, onion, cilantro, and most of the nori. Add the cooked salmon or chicken, if desired. Toss to coat; the more you toss, the creamier the dressing will become as the avocado breaks down. Season with more red pepper flakes. Just before serving, sprinkle the remaining nori on top.

Three-Herb
GREEK-BOK SALAD

I'VE ALWAYS LOVED THE WAY Greek salad tastes, but when I went dairy-free, I wondered how it would work without chunks of feta cheese. The answer? Dee-licious. I let the other salty element in the dish—briny kalamatas—fill in for the cheese, upped the herb quotient, and kept the dressing tart and tangy. I also love the textural variety I get by folding in some baby bok choy, also known as pak choy, a member of the highly nutritious cruciferous family of vegetables. In addition to its crunch, bok choy is a great source of vitamins A, C, and K. Win-win!

Serves 6

For the dressing

½ cup extra-virgin olive oil

⅓ cup fresh lemon juice

2 garlic cloves, minced

2 teaspoons chopped fresh oregano

1 teaspoon fine sea salt

1 teaspoon freshly ground black pepper

For the salad

1 romaine lettuce head or 2 romaine hearts (12 ounces total), chopped (6 cups)

3 small bunches baby bok choy, chopped (2 cups)

1 pound tomatoes (Roma, vine-ripened, beefsteak, cherry, or a combination), chopped

1 large cucumber, peeled and chopped (2 cups)

4 scallions, thinly sliced (½ cup)

¼ cup chopped kalamata olives

2 tablespoons chopped fresh mint

2 tablespoons chopped fresh dill

Make the dressing: In a large bowl, whisk together all of the ingredients.

Make the salad: Add the romaine, bok choy, tomatoes, cucumber, scallions, olives, mint, and dill to the dressing. Toss and serve.

HEALTH-HELPING KELP NOODLE SALAD
with Tamarind Dressing

A SWEET-TART ADDITION TO SAUCES and dressings, tamarind paste—extracted from a pod-like fruit that looks sort of like a caterpillar—is available at Asian, South American, and specialty markets but is often packaged with preservatives and other additives, like citric acid, that I find distasteful. So I make my own. Though tamarind does contain carbohydrates, its benefits—phenolic antioxidants, vitamins B and C—more than make up for them. There's some work involved in making the paste (it was hard for me the first few times), but the results—a pure, tangy product with multiple uses—sure is worth it. You'll have leftover paste; toss it into stir-fries or curries for extra zing.

Next: kelp noodles! You'll do a double take when you check the nutrition label on this product, typically found at health food stores or online. Since they're made from little more than kelp and a natural binder, they've got virtually no calories and only 1 gram of carbs per serving, making them a worthy contender for the noodle championship. Though they can be stir-fried, I find they work best in cold salads like this one, with a market basket's worth of raw veggies and a compelling dressing.

Serves 4 to 6

¼ cup Pure Tamarind Paste (recipe follows)

6 tablespoons coconut aminos (see page 26)

3 garlic cloves, minced

1 tablespoon finely minced peeled fresh ginger

Finely grated zest and juice of 1 lime

2 teaspoons bottled Asian chili garlic sauce or sambal oelek

1 (12-ounce) package kelp noodles, (see above), such as Sea Tangle brand, rinsed, drained, separated, and fluffed

1 large carrot, peeled and shredded (I like to use a julienne peeler)

1 large red bell pepper, thinly sliced

1¼ cups snow peas, trimmed and left whole or thinly sliced

½ cup sliced fresh basil leaves

¼ cup packed fresh cilantro leaves

In a large bowl, whisk the tamarind paste with the coconut aminos, garlic, ginger, lime zest and juice, and chili garlic sauce. Add the kelp noodles, carrot, bell pepper, snow peas, basil, and cilantro and toss. Serve immediately.

Pure Tamarind Paste

Makes ¾ cup

1 pound tamarind pods (in shell)

2 cups water

Using your hands, remove the shells from the tamarind pods, taking out as many small bits of shell as possible. Place the tamarind pods (including the seeds) and the water in a 2-quart saucepan. Bring to a boil, reduce the heat, and simmer, pressing down occasionally with a silicone spatula to dislodge the seeds, until a thick liquid has formed (the texture will resemble canned tomato sauce). Using a food mill or a fine-mesh strainer, strain the solids from the tamarind paste; discard the solids. Store the paste in the refrigerator in an airtight container for up to 3 weeks.

KALE, KALE CHIP, AND PEPITA SALAD
with Goldenberry Dressing

THIS DOUBLE-KALE SALAD BENEFITS FROM three kinds of crunch: raw kale, crunchy kale chips, and pepitas. It's tossed with a dressing of oil, vinegar, and my homemade mustard, with a sweet and tangy element derived from a surprising source—goldenberries.

————Serves 6————

For the goldenberry dressing

½ cup goldenberries (see page 26)

½ cup extra-virgin olive oil

3 tablespoons unfiltered apple cider vinegar

1 teaspoon Grainy Mustard (page 104)

1 teaspoon dried (not ground) eleuthero (see page 26)

1 garlic clove, peeled

¼ teaspoon freshly ground black pepper

For the salad

1 large head dinosaur (lacinato) or curly kale, very thinly shredded

⅓ cup pepitas, soaked and dehydrated (see page 32)

1 large shallot, very thinly sliced

2 cups kale chips, store-bought or homemade (page 230), crumbled

Make the goldenberry dressing: Soak the goldenberries in warm water until softened, 2 hours. Drain and discard the liquid. In a blender, puree the berries, oil, vinegar, mustard, eleuthero, garlic, and pepper until smooth.

Make the salad: In a large bowl, toss the kale, pepitas, and shallot with the dressing. Top with the kale chips and serve immediately.

Peanut-Free
THAI NOODLE SALAD

HERE'S ONE OF THE RECIPES that make people think I'm a kitchen pro. Sweet, tangy, savory, rich, and crunchy, it ups the ante on all those peanut-noodle salads that you've wanted to love over the years but—let's face it—are usually too sweet or so gloppy, they could glue your mouth shut! Using pineapple to help sweeten the sauce reduces the amount of sweetener necessary; add the protein of your choice if you want, but the dish is super-satisfying as is. A special shout-out is warranted here to chef Dacia Horn at my kids' school. I first tasted a version of this dressing when she made it for school lunch—it was so popular that faculty and parents began asking for it.

————————Serves 6 to 8————————

For the peanut-free dressing

1¼ cups very ripe, juicy fresh pineapple chunks

½ cup coconut palm sugar (see page 29)

6 tablespoons coconut aminos (see page 26)

¼ cup water

3 tablespoons fresh lime juice

1 tablespoon untoasted sesame oil

1 (3-inch) piece fresh ginger, peeled and coarsely chopped

1 (2-inch) piece fresh turmeric, peeled and coarsely chopped

2 tablespoons minced garlic (divided)

2 tablespoons extra-virgin olive oil

1 medium onion, chopped

1 cup sunflower seed butter, store-bought or homemade (page 97)

For the salad

1 medium head Napa cabbage, chopped

1 (5-ounce) bag baby spinach, chopped

2 large carrots, peeled and julienned

1 large cucumber, unpeeled, sliced as thinly as possible

2 cups fresh herbs, such as mint, cilantro, or flat-leaf parsley, finely chopped

½ large red onion, very thinly sliced

Cooked chicken strips (optional)

Gomasio (see page 26), for garnish

Organic rice noodles, cooked, or kelp noodles (see page 27), such as Sea Tangle brand, rinsed, drained, separated, and fluffed (optional), for serving

Make the dressing: In a blender, combine the pineapple, coconut sugar, coconut aminos, water, lime juice, sesame oil, ginger, turmeric, and 1 tablespoon of the garlic. Blend until smooth.

In a large skillet, heat the olive oil over medium heat. Add the onion and cook, stirring occasionally, until softened and golden, 9 to 10 minutes. Add the remaining 1 tablespoon garlic and cook for 1 minute. Reduce the heat to medium-low, add the blended dressing and cook until warmed through, 2 to 3 minutes. Whisk in the sunflower seed butter and cook until thickened and warmed through, 1 to 2 minutes. Remove from the heat and cover to keep warm.

Make the salad: In a large bowl, toss the cabbage, spinach, carrots, cucumber, herbs, and red onion. Add the dressing and the chicken strips, if using, and toss well to coat. Garnish with the gomasio. Serve with rice noodles or kelp noodles, if desired.

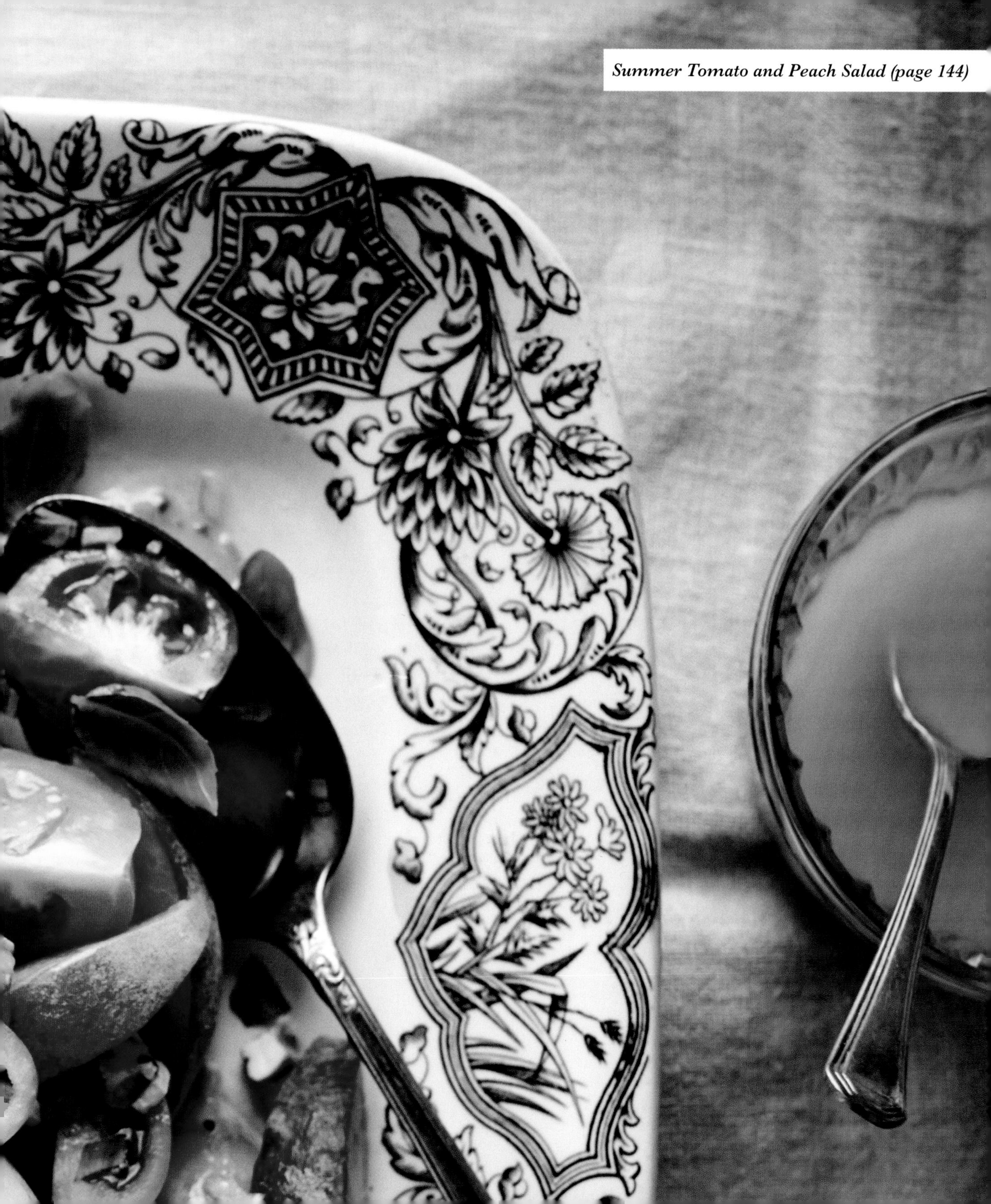

Summer Tomato and Peach Salad (page 144)

SUMMER TOMATO AND PEACH SALAD
with Pickled Red Onion, Fresh Herbs, and Walnuts

THIS IS ONE OF THOSE DISHES you should make only in the summertime, when produce is at its peak in both flavor and nutritional value. The combination of peaches and tomatoes is special, and the addition of the quick pickles is show-offy, yet easy. It's fun watching the red onion rings turn a bright shade of vermilion as they pickle. With a double dose of walnuts—both nuts and oil—this is a salad you can really feel good about. (See photo pages 142–143.)

Serves 6

For the pickled onion

1½ cups unfiltered apple cider vinegar

⅓ cup maple syrup or coconut palm sugar (see page 29)

5 black peppercorns

1 bay leaf

¼ teaspoon fine sea salt

1 large red onion, sliced into thin rings (about 2 cups)

For the dressing

3 tablespoons unfiltered apple cider vinegar

1 small shallot, finely minced

½ teaspoon Grainy Mustard (page 104)

½ teaspoon fine sea salt

¼ teaspoon freshly ground black pepper

½ cup walnut oil

For the salad

3 large heirloom tomatoes, sliced into wedges

2 ripe peaches, unpeeled, pitted and sliced into wedges

¼ cup sliced fresh basil

2 tablespoons chopped fresh tarragon

¼ cup walnuts, soaked and dehydrated (see page 32), chopped

Make the pickled onion: In a small saucepan, bring the vinegar, maple syrup, peppercorns, bay leaf, and salt to a boil. Add the onion and cook for about 1 minute. Remove from the heat and let the onion sit in the liquid for 10 minutes. Drain the liquid from the onion, reserving the liquid, and let the onion and liquid cool to room temperature separately. Place the onion in a jar, cover with the liquid, seal, and refrigerate until chilled. The pickled onion will keep in the refrigerator for up to 2 weeks.

Make the dressing: In a small bowl or blender, whisk or blend together the vinegar, shallot, mustard, salt, and pepper. Whisk or blend in the walnut oil in a slow stream until the dressing is creamy and emulsified.

Make the salad: Arrange the tomato and peach wedges on a pretty platter, then arrange some of the pickled onion on top. Drizzle with the dressing, sprinkle the basil, tarragon, and walnuts on top, and serve.

MULTI-HERB AND HEMP SEED TABBOULEH
with Garlic-Lime Dressing

TABBOULEH IS TYPICALLY MADE WITH bulgur, but here hemp seeds heroically stand in as a heart-healthy, gluten-free option. Most tabbouleh dressings contain lemon juice, but I switch it up here with lime, which adds an altogether different zing. If you can't find packaged edible flowers, use pesticide-free nasturtiums, rose petals, or violets.

————————Serves 6————————

For the dressing

⅓ cup fresh lime or lemon juice

⅓ cup extra-virgin olive oil

2 garlic cloves, minced

½ teaspoon fine sea salt

¼ teaspoon freshly ground black pepper

For the salad

2 cups chopped fresh flat-leaf parsley

1 cup chopped watercress

1 cup chopped fresh dill

1 cup chopped fresh chives

¾ cup chopped fresh mint

½ cup thinly sliced scallions

½ cup chopped fresh cilantro

1 (1-ounce) package edible flowers, gently chopped

1 cup hemp seeds, soaked and dehydrated (see page 32)

Make the dressing: In a large bowl, whisk together all of the ingredients until emulsified.

Make the salad: Add all of the salad ingredients to the bowl with the dressing, toss to combine, and serve.

TIP The secret to this salad is its bounty of chopped fresh herbs. Running over the herbs too many times with your knife wets and blackens them, so wash and dry them well before chopping and use a very sharp blade and a light touch.

Eggless, Dairy-Free
CAESAR SALAD
with Sea Cracker Croutons

HAIL, CAESAR! This salad is an oft-requested favorite, mainly because it tastes just like the restaurant version without leaving you weighted down and greased out. You'll find it hard to believe that the dressing contains no eggs or dairy whatsoever. Creamy almond milk forms the base, and nutritional yeast—something I use only in moderation—really does approximate the savory goodness of Parmigiano-Reggiano cheese. I add anchovies to the dressing instead of keeping it vegan because I love the boost of omega-3s the fish provides, not to mention that authentic, tossed-at-the-tableside flavor. If you aren't doing fish, simply omit the anchovies—no harm. Though they're not traditional, I add avocados and carrot to the salad for extra raw goodness. And instead of croutons, I use Two Moms in the Raw Sea Crackers, which add crunch to every mouthful.

—————————*Serves 6 to 8*—————————

1 (1-pound) bag romaine lettuce hearts, chopped

2 cups halved cherry tomatoes

2 avocados, pitted, peeled, and sliced

½ small red onion, thinly sliced

1 medium carrot, peeled and grated or cut into matchsticks or coins

1 cup Eggless, Dairy-Free Caesar Dressing (recipe follows)

1 cup crumbled Two Moms in the Raw Sea Crackers, flaxseeds, or crumbled nori (seaweed), for serving

In a large bowl, combine the romaine, tomatoes, avocados, onion, carrot, and dressing and toss lightly. Serve with the crackers, flaxseeds, or nori on the side, encouraging people to add them like croutons just before eating.

Eggless, Dairy-Free Caesar Dressing

——————*Makes about 2 cups*——————

½ cup Raw-mond Milk (page 35) or
other unsweetened almond milk

Juice of 2 lemons

2 garlic cloves, minced

2 tablespoons nutritional yeast

1 or 2 oil-packed anchovy fillets, drained

1 teaspoon fine sea salt,
plus more to taste

¼ teaspoon mustard powder

⅛ teaspoon freshly ground black pepper

1 cup extra-virgin olive oil

In a blender or food processor, combine the almond milk, lemon juice, garlic, yeast, anchovy, salt, mustard powder, and pepper and blend on high until incorporated, about 5 seconds. With the machine still running, drizzle in the oil in a steady stream until emulsified; the dressing will be thick, but not as thick as mayonnaise. Season with additional salt. Leftover dressing can be refrigerated in an airtight container for up to 5 days.

RAW TATSOI AND PLUM SALAD
with Hemp Oil Dressing

THE BENEFITS OF HEMP SEED OIL are many, among them a megadose of ALA (alpha-linolenic acid), which converts into two heart-healthy omega-3s in the body, and possibly has cholesterol-lowering properties—and did I mention its being a catalyst for world peace? To temper its slightly bitter flavor, I cut it with olive oil here and add a touch of sweetness. The dressing's flavor is further balanced by the earthiness of tatsoi, a cruciferous green increasingly available at farmers' markets that tastes like a cross between spinach and bok choy. Juicy plum segments are a pretty finish.

—————————Serves 6—————————

For the dressing

¼ cup extra-virgin olive oil

2 tablespoons hemp seed oil

3 tablespoons unfiltered
apple cider vinegar

2 tablespoons finely chopped
fresh flat-leaf parsley

2 tablespoons thinly sliced scallion

2 teaspoons coconut palm sugar (see
page 29) or 3 drops stevia sweetener

¼ teaspoon fine sea salt

¼ teaspoon freshly ground black pepper

Pinch of cayenne pepper

For the salad

2 bunches tatsoi, chopped

1 shallot, very thinly sliced

1 red bell pepper, cut into strips

1 large carrot, peeled and grated

2 ripe, juicy plums, pitted
and cut into wedges

Make the dressing: In a medium bowl, whisk together all of the dressing ingredients until emulsified.

Make the salad: To the dressing, add the tatsoi, shallot, bell pepper, and carrot and toss. Top with the plum wedges just before serving.

TIP For a warm salad, cook the tatsoi, stirring, for 1 to 2 minutes in coconut oil (see page 23). Bok choy can be subbed for the tatsoi.

ENDIVE, APPLE, AND RED ONION SALAD

THIS SALAD CONTAINS SOME of my favorite things: mildly bitter endive (a great source of vitamin K and folate), sweet, crunchy apples, and sharp red onion. The fragrant, walnut oil–based dressing turns this into an elegant little salad, perfect for pairing with any chicken or fish dish.

—————————Serves 6—————————

¼ cup walnut oil

2 tablespoons unfiltered apple cider vinegar

2 teaspoons Grainy Mustard (page 104)

2 teaspoons coconut palm sugar (see page 29) or pure maple syrup

⅛ teaspoon fine sea salt

4 heads Belgian endive, thinly sliced

2 crisp, red apples, such as Pink Lady or Fuji, cut into matchsticks

½ small red onion, thinly sliced

4 cups baby arugula

½ cup walnuts, soaked and dehydrated (see page 32), chopped

In a large bowl, whisk together the oil, vinegar, mustard, coconut palm sugar, and salt. Add the endive, apples, and onion and toss with the dressing. Arrange the arugula on a serving platter and top with the tossed salad. Garnish with the walnuts and serve.

GARDEN JEWEL SALAD

THIS SALAD IS A FEAST for all of the senses, something that's essential for me given my CADD (Cooking Attention Deficit Disorder), an undocumented, but very real, phenomenon. Brown makes me feel down, and this salad is anything but. Gorgeous hues of deep purple, red, pink, and green are a rainbow for both plate and palate. Anyone who thinks winter is a fresh-produce dead zone has never tasted this salad, with its perfect balance of seasonal goodies and light, citrusy dressing.

———————————*Serves 8*———————————

4 medium beets, scrubbed and dried

3 tablespoons plus 4 teaspoons extra-virgin olive oil

Fine sea salt and freshly ground black pepper to taste

1 large head butter lettuce, cut into bite-sized pieces

1 large or 2 small fennel bulbs, stalks and tough core discarded, thinly sliced, fronds reserved for garnish

1 large grapefruit, segmented, juice reserved

2 large, firm, ripe avocados, pitted, peeled, and cut into wedges

½ cup pomegranate seeds

2 tablespoons coarsely chopped fresh dill

Juice of 1 lime

1½ teaspoons pure maple syrup

1 teaspoon Grainy Mustard (page 104)

Preheat the oven to 400°F.

Place each beet on a separate 8-inch square of parchment paper, drizzle each with 1 teaspoon of the oil, and season with salt and pepper to taste. Wrap each beet in the parchment and place on a baking sheet. Roast until tender-firm, 65 to 70 minutes. Remove from the oven and cool completely. Using a paper towel, slip the skins from the beets and discard, then cut the beets into wedges.

Arrange the lettuce on a platter, then top with the beets, fennel, grapefruit, avocados, pomegranate seeds, and dill.

In a bowl, whisk together the reserved grapefruit juice, the lime juice, the remaining 3 tablespoons oil, the maple syrup, mustard, and salt and pepper. Drizzle the dressing on the salad and lightly toss to incorporate. Garnish with the fennel fronds.

TIP How do you segment a grapefruit (or an orange)? It's kind of a pain. If you must be super chef-y, you could a) cut off the top and bottom of the grapefruit to create flat surfaces; b) cut the peel and pith off the grapefruit, following the shape of the fruit as closely as possible; then c) cut between the membranes, releasing the segments into a bowl and catching the extra juice. Or you could just do steps a) and b), then cut the grapefruit into ½-inch-thick disks.

ORANGE AND BERMUDA ONION SALAD

MY MOTHER-IN-LAW, KNOWN AS OMA, created this sunny salad. Though you can eat this baby right after it's dressed, letting the greens wilt, the onions collapse in on themselves, and the flavors meld makes for an even more awesome bowl of greens. Other than the natural sugar from the oranges and a couple drops of stevia sweetener, there's nothing sugary here, making this a good option when you're trying to keep your glycemic index as low as possible.

————————*Serves 6*————————

6 cups salad greens of your choice, such as spinach, arugula, romaine, or watercress

2 oranges, segmented (see Tip, page 154), juice reserved

1 cup very thinly sliced Bermuda, Vidalia, or red onion

2 tablespoons extra-virgin olive oil

2 tablespoons unfiltered apple cider vinegar

2 or 3 drops stevia sweetener (optional)

⅛ teaspoon fine sea salt

⅛ teaspoon freshly ground black pepper

In a medium salad bowl, layer the greens, orange segments, and onion. Whisk together the reserved orange juice, oil, vinegar, stevia (if using), salt, and pepper. Pour over the salad, cover loosely, and let it sit on the counter until the greens are wilted, at least 2 hours and up to 8. Uncover, toss, and serve.

CRISPY BRUSSELS SPROUT, POMEGRANATE SEED, AND TENDER GREENS SALAD

THIS SIMPLE DISH STANDS IN for a meaty main course on many an evening at my house. With the crispy, browned edges of the Brussels sprouts, the juicy burst of sweet pomegranate seeds, the tender greens, and the herbalicious dressing, it's a winner of a dinner. Don't take my word for it: Make it and find out for yourself.

——————Serves 4 to 6——————

3 tablespoons extra-virgin olive oil

1½ pounds Brussels sprouts, trimmed and chopped

5 ounces tender salad greens of your choice

¾ cup pomegranate seeds

½ recipe Herb Dressing (page 126)

In a very large (12-inch) skillet or two medium skillets, heat the oil over medium-high heat. Add the Brussels sprouts and cook, being careful not to disturb until the underside is browned and crisp, 3 to 4 minutes. Stir the sprouts and continue cooking until tender but not mushy, 2 to 3 minutes. Remove from the heat.

Arrange the salad greens on a platter, top with the Brussels sprouts and pomegranate seeds, drizzle with the dressing, and serve.

Pomegranate Seeds

Pomegranate seeds are bursting with nutrients, thanks in large part to a particularly potent antioxidant polyphenols. Pomegranates are in season from fall to midwinter. Seek them out to benefit from their burst of tart crimson juice, not to mention vitamin C, potassium, and fiber.

SHAVED BRUSSELS SPROUT SALAD
with Lemony Lucuma Dressing

I CAN'T GET ENOUGH OF LEMON in salad dressings—it seems to enhance the crunchiness and bring out the distinct flavors of a variety of lettuces and vegetables. The real revelation here, though, is the Peruvian lucuma powder used to both thicken and sweeten the dressing. Rich in niacin and beta carotene, lucuma is a superfood fruit that provides a nifty way to get rid of some, or all, of the sugar in a recipe. The natural inulin fiber in the optional coconut nectar encourages digestive health. And the salad itself? Perfection! The crunch of walnuts and two kinds of cruciferous veggies, the sweet, chewy dates, and the juicy, vitamin-packed citrus combine to create something special. I can think of few things I'd rather eat on a wintry afternoon—or anytime, for that matter.

————————*Serves 6*————————

For the dressing

½ cup extra-virgin olive oil

3 tablespoons fresh lemon juice

1 tablespoon blood orange
or regular orange juice

2 teaspoons lucuma powder
(see page 27)

1 tablespoon finely minced shallot

2 teaspoons pure maple syrup or
coconut nectar (see page 29; optional)

¼ teaspoon fine sea salt

⅛ teaspoon freshly ground black pepper

For the salad

1½ pounds Brussels sprouts,
trimmed and thinly shaved with a
mandoline slicer or food processor

6 dinosaur (lacinato) kale leaves,
thinly shredded crosswise

2 blood or Cara Cara oranges,
segmented (see Tip, page 154),
juice reserved for dressing

1 large shallot, very thinly sliced

6 Medjool dates, pitted and chopped

¼ cup walnuts, soaked and dehydrated
(see page 32), chopped

Make the dressing: In a large bowl, whisk together the oil, lemon juice, orange juice, lucuma, shallot, maple syrup (if using), salt, and pepper, as well as the reserved juice from the oranges, until creamy or blend in a blender for 15 seconds.

Make the salad: Add all of the ingredients to the bowl with the dressing. Toss well to combine. Serve immediately or let sit at room temperature to wilt for up to 1 hour.

CHAPTER 6

veggie mains

Whoever said you need meat to anchor a dinner hasn't eaten at my house, where many nights dinner consists of a plant-based main course. These veggiecentric dishes are designed to make believers out of even the most reluctant eaters. The best part? You'll feel as good the next day as you do while you're eating them.

the recipes

VEGGIE BURGERS

DEPENDING ON THE DAY, I will "cheat-eat" quinoa. Here I use it to create a meatless "burger" the kids love, but since there's only 1 cup quinoa in this whole recipe, my conscience remains intact. I use a bit of nutritional yeast to up the savory taste of the burgers, but feel free to leave it out if you're being extra-vigilant about Candida.

—————————Serves 8 to 10—————————

½ head cauliflower, trimmed, core and head, finely chopped (about 3 cups)

5 tablespoons extra-virgin olive oil (divided)

2 teaspoons fine sea salt (divided)

½ teaspoon freshly ground black pepper (divided)

1 medium onion, finely chopped

3 garlic cloves, minced

1 pound maitake mushrooms, finely chopped

1 cup cooked red quinoa (see page 33)

1 cup finely chopped kale

½ cup chopped fresh flat-leaf parsley

¼ cup hemp seeds, soaked and dehydrated (see page 32)

3 large eggs, lightly beaten

½ cup flax meal

2 tablespoons nutritional yeast (optional)

1 tablespoon chia seeds, finely ground in a spice grinder

Lettuce leaves, for serving (optional)

Preheat the oven to 400°F.

In a large bowl, toss the cauliflower with 2 tablespoons of the oil, 1 teaspoon of the salt, and ¼ teaspoon of the pepper. Spread on a large baking sheet and roast until the cauliflower is browned and has shrunken slightly, 20 to 25 minutes.

Meanwhile, in a large skillet, heat 2 tablespoons of the oil over medium-high heat. Add the onion and cook, stirring, until tender, 7 to 8 minutes. Add the garlic and cook for 1 minute. Add the mushrooms and cook, stirring, until they release some of their water, 4 to 5 minutes.

Transfer the cauliflower and the onion-mushroom mixture to a large bowl and add the quinoa, kale, parsley, hemp seeds, eggs, flax meal, nutritional yeast (if using), chia seeds, the remaining 1 teaspoon salt, and the remaining ¼ teaspoon pepper. Mix well to combine. With damp hands, form the mixture into 8 to 10 equal-sized patties.

Heat a large nonstick skillet over medium-high heat and add the remaining 1 tablespoon oil. Working in batches, cook the burgers until browned, 4 to 5 minutes per side. To bake, arrange the burgers on a parchment-lined baking sheet and bake until golden, 20 to 22 minutes. Wrap in lettuce leaves to serve, if desired.

SPAGHETTI MARAWNARA

I LOVE A GOOD COOKED SPAGHETTI SAUCE as much as the next person, but this raw version has several advantages over it, most notably that you can make it faster than your kids can complain there's nothing in the fridge for dinner. Just throw everything in the blender and voilà! I've added some sun-dried tomatoes to the mix here; believe it or not, they contain more cancer-fighting lycopene than their raw originals. I eat tomatoes only in moderation, since they're fairly high in sugar.

—————————*Makes 3 cups*—————————

6 large Roma or 4 vine-ripened tomatoes, coarsely chopped

3 garlic cloves, minced

1 medium shallot, chopped

2 oil-packed sun-dried tomatoes, drained and chopped

1 teaspoon fine sea salt

5 large fresh basil leaves

2 teaspoons chopped fresh oregano

3 tablespoons extra-virgin olive oil

4 cups lightly cooked zucchini ribbons or cooked spaghetti squash or organic rice noodles, for serving

Combine all of the ingredients, except the zucchini, squash, or rice noodles, in a blender and pulse until you reach the desired consistency.

Serve with the zucchini ribbons, spaghetti squash, or rice noodles.

SQUASHED SPAGHETTI AND SWISS CHARD
with Fresh Tomato Sauce

MY MOM, MARSHA, turned me on to spaghetti squash as a kid. Rarely has something so unassuming on the outside been so cool-looking inside. Once you take a fork to cooked spaghetti squash, it turns into the most delightfully textured squiggles that take to sauce just as noodles do. Though there are trace amounts of healthy vitamins and minerals, the main nutritional benefit of spaghetti squash is fiber—and the surprisingly low amount of sugar per serving. By swapping in the squash for starchy noodles of any kind, you'll be lightening your glycemic load without sacrificing feeling full at the end of the meal. Since I love the way the stress-busting ashwagandha blends in with the flavor of other herbs, I sneak some into the sauce.

————————Serves 4 to 6————————

For the squash

1 large spaghetti squash

2 tablespoons extra-virgin olive oil (divided)

1½ teaspoons fine sea salt (divided)

½ teaspoon freshly ground black pepper (divided)

6 large rainbow chard leaves, stems chopped and reserved for sauce, leaves cut into thin ribbons

For the fresh tomato sauce

2 tablespoons extra-virgin olive oil

1 large onion, chopped

Reserved chopped chard stems

6 garlic cloves, minced

2½ pounds vine-ripened tomatoes, chopped

6 or 7 oil-packed sun-dried tomatoes, drained and chopped

½ cup thinly sliced fresh basil, plus more for garnish

1 tablespoon chopped fresh oregano

2 teaspoons ashwagandha (see page 25)

1 teaspoon fine sea salt

¼ teaspoon freshly ground black pepper

¼ teaspoon red pepper flakes

Roast the squash: Preheat the oven to 400°F.

Split the spaghetti squash lengthwise, brush the cut sides with 1 tablespoon of the oil, and sprinkle with 1 teaspoon salt and ¼ teaspoon pepper. Arrange the squash

cut side down on a baking sheet and bake until the shell of the squash can be easily pierced with a fork or metal skewer, 35 to 40 minutes.

Meanwhile, make the fresh tomato sauce: In a medium saucepan, heat the oil over medium-high heat. Add the onion and cook, stirring, until translucent, about 6 minutes. Add the chard stems and garlic and cook for about 2 minutes. Add the tomatoes, sun-dried tomatoes, basil, oregano, ashwagandha, salt, pepper, and red pepper flakes and bring to a boil. Reduce the heat, cover, and simmer until the sauce thickens, about 15 minutes.

Assemble the dish: When the squash is done, scrape the squash strands from the shells and toss with the chard ribbons, the remaining 1 tablespoon oil, the remaining ½ teaspoon salt, and the remaining ¼ teaspoon pepper. Arrange the squash mixture on a platter, top with the sauce, and garnish with basil.

TIP Eat This! Sun-Dried Tomatoes

In addition to adding a salty, savory touch to food, sun-dried tomatoes contain a significant amount of fiber, lycopene (a cancer-fighting carotene), protein, potassium, iron, B vitamins, and vitamin K, essential for bone and blood health.

Roasting Spaghetti Squash Seeds

When you hollow out your spaghetti squash, don't throw out the seeds! Instead, bake them up into a fab snack that's extra-crunchy.

In a bowl, cover the scraped seeds with water. Cover, refrigerate, and soak for 12 hours.

To dehydrate: Arrange the prepared seeds on nonstick dehydrator sheets (see page 36) and dehydrate at 188°F, stirring every 6 hours, for 18 to 24 hours, until crisped.

To bake: Preheat the oven to 350°F. Using your fingers, rub the seeds to dislodge any squash fibers. Pour off the liquid and dry the seeds with a towel. Wipe out the bowl, return the seeds to the bowl, and toss with a bit of olive oil or melted coconut oil and salt and pepper to taste (you can also add dried herbs and cayenne pepper—or go sweet by adding a touch of maple syrup, cinnamon, and nutmeg). Arrange the seeds on parchment-lined baking sheets and bake until golden and fragrant, 20 to 22 minutes. Cool completely, then snack to your heart's content!

GREEN CURRY
in a Hurry

A GOOD, THAI-STYLE CURRY IS a great dinner option, and my kids love its combination of creamy, sweet, salty, and spicy elements. Store-bought green curry paste—full of preservatives and with muted flavors—doesn't live up to the promise of its raw ingredients. My version, which serves as the basis for a one-pan coconut curry, will turn everything you thought you knew about green curry on its ear. Fresh hot peppers, handfuls of herbs, and loads of antioxidant-rich components come together with a brightness and depth of flavor that knocks my family's socks off every time. Use or freeze the curry paste soon after making it; its flavors fade with every day it sits in the fridge.

————————Serves 4 to 6————————

5 cups cubed eggplant

Fine sea salt and freshly ground black pepper

3 tablespoons coconut oil (divided; see page 23)

3 shallots, thinly sliced

6 garlic cloves, thinly sliced

1 tablespoon chopped peeled fresh ginger

2 medium carrots, peeled and cut into coins

1 red bell pepper, cut into strips

1 yellow bell pepper, cut into strips

3 cups broccoli florets (from 1 small head)

2½ cups (about 1½ cans) coconut milk

⅔ cup Green Curry Paste (recipe follows), plus more to taste

2 tablespoons coconut palm sugar (see page 29)

¼ cup chopped fresh cilantro

¼ cup chopped fresh mint

¼ cup chopped fresh basil

Lime wedges, for serving

Season the eggplant generously with salt and pepper. In a wok or large skillet, heat 1 tablespoon of the coconut oil over medium-high heat. Add the eggplant and cook, stirring occasionally, until browned, just cooked through, and tender but still firm, 4 to 5 minutes. Remove the eggplant from the pan with a slotted spoon and reserve.

Add the remaining 2 tablespoons coconut oil to the pan, then add the shallots, garlic, and ginger and cook, stirring, until softened and fragrant, 1 to 2 minutes. Add the carrots, bell peppers, and broccoli and cook until crisp-tender, 1 to 2 minutes.

Return the eggplant to the pan, then add the coconut milk, curry paste, and coconut palm sugar. Bring to a boil, reduce the heat, and simmer until the liquid thickens,

2 to 3 minutes. Remove from the heat, add more curry paste, and stir in the cilantro, mint, and basil. Divide among bowls and serve with the lime wedges.

Green Curry Paste

SINCE THIS RECIPE MAKES EXTRA paste, you can freeze it in ice cube trays, then pop out 5 cubes (about ⅔ cup) per recipe. That way, the next three times you want to make curry, it's in a hurry. If you prefer a hotter curry, leave the jalapeño seeds in. The kaffir lime leaves, common in Southeast Asian cooking, can be found fresh at Indian or Asian markets; dried versions are available in better grocery stores or online.

————————Makes 2 cups————————

2 jalapeños, seeded (optional) and coarsely chopped

1 small bunch fresh cilantro, stalks included

2 fresh lemongrass stalks

1 (2-inch) piece fresh ginger, peeled

1 (1-inch) piece fresh turmeric, peeled

4 garlic cloves, peeled

2 shallots, coarsely chopped

4 fresh or dried kaffir lime leaves (see page 27)

2 teaspoons whole coriander seeds

1 teaspoon black peppercorns or freshly ground black pepper

1 teaspoon cumin seeds or ground cumin

¼ cup water, plus more if needed

½ teaspoon fine sea salt

Combine all of the ingredients in a blender and puree until smooth, adding additional water by the tablespoonful if necessary. Transfer to a bowl and reserve. Cover and refrigerate the curry paste if you're not using it right away.

The curry paste can be frozen in standard ice cube trays; once frozen, transfer the cubes to a Ziploc bag. The frozen paste will keep for up to 3 months.

Each cube yields about 2 tablespoons curry paste, which can be defrosted and used as needed.

CAULIFLOWER SANDWICH WRAP OR PIZZA CRUST
(with Choice of Toppings)

CAULIFLOWER-BASED CRUSTS HAVE BEEN POPPING UP all over the place, and I have to admit that I was skeptical about them—until I tried one for myself. You'll marvel at how the dough forms easily in the food processor, aided by the elasticity that healthy flax meal, almond meal, and a touch of psyllium husk provide. It makes a flavorful crust for pizza and a great sandwich wrap, encasing any filling you throw its way with ease. Reheated in the oven to a crisper state, it acts as a great base crust for a pizza or flatbread-like creation.

Makes 10 to 11 wraps or 6 (6-inch) crusts

1½ pounds (6 cups) cauliflower florets (from a 2-pound head)

½ cup water, plus more if necessary

5 tablespoons almond meal or almond flour (see page 260)

¼ cup flax meal

2 tablespoons Italian seasoning

2 teaspoons psyllium husk (see page 27)

2 garlic cloves, finely minced

2 teaspoons fine sea salt

1 teaspoon ground dried eleuthero (see page 26)

Olive oil cooking spray

Preheat the oven to 400°F.

Place the cauliflower florets in a food processor, add the water, and puree until small pieces form, scraping down the sides of the processor and adding water by the tablespoonful if necessary until smooth, 45 to 60 seconds. Add the almond meal, flax meal, Italian seasoning, psyllium husk, garlic, salt, and eleuthero and process until incorporated, 5 to 10 seconds.

Line baking sheets with parchment paper and coat with cooking spray.

Using ⅓ cup batter at a time, spread the batter into thin disks about 9 inches in diameter for large and 5 inches for small. Bake until the batter dries out and the edges are slightly golden, 17 minutes for large and 15 minutes for small. Remove the parchment sheets to cooling racks, cool the wraps completely, and peel them from the parchment. The wraps can be stored between layers of parchment in the refrigerator for up to 3 days.

To rebake: Return the wraps to oven to 350°F for 7 to 10 minutes until crisp.

Toppings

- For a salad pizza, top with Marawnara sauce (page 164) and lightly dressed greens.
- Spread with Creamy Olive and Artichoke Dip (page 96) and top with chopped olives and sun-dried tomatoes.
- Spread with Roasted Garlic, Pepita, and Cilantro Pesto (page 88) and top with slices of Za'atar and Lemon Grilled Chicken (page 199).

VEGGIE SHISH KEBABS
with Chimichurri Sauce

CHIMICHURRI IS AN ARGENTINIAN CONDIMENT usually served with steak, but it's a worthy match for these veggie skewers, which are so substantial, you won't miss the beef. You might be tempted to toss everything in the blender, but this is one instance when hand-chopping all of the elements makes a big difference in the texture of the finished product. Aim for the consistency of a loose, chunky pesto, and you're on the right track.

—Serves 4 to 6 (makes 12 skewers)—

For the chimichurri

2 scallions, thinly sliced

1 cup loosely packed fresh flat-leaf parsley, finely chopped

½ cup loosely packed fresh cilantro, finely chopped

¼ cup loosely packed fresh mint, finely chopped

4 teaspoons chopped garlic

½ cup extra-virgin olive oil

½ teaspoon fine sea salt

For the shish kebabs

Assorted vegetables, such as cherry tomatoes; zucchini, cut into 1-inch cubes; red onion, cut into 1-inch chunks; multicolored bell peppers, cut into 1-inch chunks; and maitake mushrooms, cut into 1-inch chunks

Extra-virgin olive oil

Fine sea salt and freshly ground black pepper

Make the chimichurri: In a medium bowl, combine all of the ingredients until well mixed. Set aside

Make the shish kebabs: If using wooden skewers, soak them in water for 30 minutes before using. String 5 or 6 vegetable pieces on each of twelve 6- or 8-inch skewers, trying to arrange them so that the skewers will sit evenly on a flat surface (this helps the vegetables cook consistently). Brush the skewers with olive oil and sprinkle with salt and pepper to taste. Arrange the skewers in a baking dish.

Marinate the kebabs: Pour half of the chimichurri on the vegetables, rotating to coat all sides. Marinate for at least 30 minutes and up to 4 hours, turning occasionally.

Cook the kebabs: Heat a grill or grill pan over medium-high heat. Grill the skewers until the vegetables are charred and tender but not mushy, 3 to 4 minutes per side. Serve the skewers with the remaining chimichurri.

QUINOA FRIED "RICE"

FRIED RICE: GOOD. MSG, low-quality soy sauce, and other icky stuff: bad. That's why I've taken to making my own fried "rice" at home, except I use healthier quinoa (a once-in-a-while food) in lieu of rice and coconut aminos in lieu of soy. The protein in quinoa transforms this from a side to a main; if you want to keep it vegan, simply omit the eggs. Though I've recommended my favorite combination of veggies, do your thing and make it your own.

—————Serves 6—————

¼ cup coconut oil (divided; see page 23)

4 large eggs, lightly beaten (optional)

1 cup thinly sliced scallions, plus more for garnish

2 tablespoons finely minced peeled fresh ginger

6 garlic cloves, minced

2 cups broccoli florets

1 yellow summer squash, finely diced

1 red bell pepper, finely diced

4 cups cooked quinoa (see page 33)

⅓ cup coconut aminos (see page 26)

2 to 3 tablespoons gluten-free tamari (or more coconut aminos)

1 tablespoon toasted sesame oil

2 cups finely chopped kale

¼ cup chopped fresh cilantro, plus more for garnish

2 tablespoons sesame seeds

Lime or lemon wedges, for serving

Heat a wok or large skillet over medium-high heat. If using eggs, add 1 tablespoon of the coconut oil to the skillet, then add the eggs and cook, stirring, until scrambled. Transfer to a bowl and reserve.

Add the remaining 3 tablespoons coconut oil and the scallions, ginger, and garlic and cook, stirring, until fragrant, 1 to 2 minutes. Add the broccoli, squash, and bell pepper and cook, stirring, until the vegetables just begin to soften, 2 to 3 minutes.

Add the quinoa, aminos, tamari, and sesame oil and cook, stirring occasionally, until the mixture is warmed through and the quinoa has absorbed most of the liquid, 3 to 4 minutes.

Stir in the kale and cilantro and cook until the kale is just wilted, about 1 minute. Return the scrambled eggs to the pan, if using, and warm through, about 1 minute. Garnish with the sesame seeds, scallions, and cilantro and serve with lime or lemon wedges on the side.

Quinoa and Sweet Potato
FRITTERS

THESE CRISPY LITTLE ROUNDS ARE causing quite a stir in the Leidich household. My kids used to turn up their noses when they heard the word "quinoa," but now everyone agrees that these are just plain delicious. Sweet potato binds together the cooked quinoa, which crisps up in the pan to form a deeply crunchy shell. Fritters often contain tons of gluten, but there's none here; quinoa flour (available at health food stores) and flax meal take its place, and you'll never notice its absence. Serve the fritters with Smoky Rawmesco Sauce (page 100), if desired.

————Serves 4 to 6————

2 tablespoons extra-virgin olive oil, plus more for frying

1 medium onion, finely chopped

4 garlic cloves, minced

1 cup mashed cooked sweet potatoes

1 large egg, beaten

2 cups cooked quinoa (see page 33), at room temperature or chilled

¼ cup quinoa flour (see above)

¼ cup flax meal

1 cup very finely chopped dinosaur (lacinato) or curly kale

¼ cup finely minced parsley

1 teaspoon fine sea salt

½ teaspoon freshly ground black pepper

In a large nonstick skillet, heat the 2 tablespoons oil over medium-high heat. Add the onion and cook, stirring, until softened and slightly browned, about 8 minutes. Add the garlic and cook for about 1 minute. Remove from the heat. Transfer the onion mixture to a large bowl and cool slightly. Wipe out the skillet with a paper towel and set aside.

Add the sweet potato and egg to the onion mixture and stir with a fork until smooth. Add the quinoa, quinoa flour, flax meal, kale, parsley, salt, and pepper and stir well until incorporated. Cover and refrigerate for 30 minutes, if you have time. Using damp hands, form the mixture into fritters 2½ to 3 inches in diameter, using 3 to 4 tablespoons of batter at a time.

In the skillet you used to cook the onion mixture, heat about 2 tablespoons oil over medium-high heat until very hot but not smoking. Fry the fritters, 4 or 5 at a time, being sure not to overcrowd the pan or move the fritters while frying, until the underside is between golden and very dark brown and crisp, 3 to 4 minutes (you want the fritters to form a crunchy crust). Using a spatula, flip the fritters and fry the other side for 3 to 4 minutes. Add more oil between batches if necessary. Drain the fritters on paper towels and serve immediately.

Butternut Squash and Chickpea
TAGINE

MY DAUGHTER SARAH IS my toughest cooking critic, and she was a little skeptical when she walked in and caught the scent of this Moroccan-inspired dish. Watching her fall in love with it at the table made me proud; a teenager voluntarily eating her vegetables? There's a first time for everything. Tagines are usually made with some sort of animal protein, but we've kept this one strictly veggie, focusing on the dish's warm spices and rib-sticking squash and chickpeas. Legumes are usually a no-no for me, so I eat around the chickpeas. You could also omit them and up the squash by half a pound. Serve this tagine with Raw Cauliflower and Hemp "Couscous" (page 224).

————————Serves 4 to 6————————

1 medium butternut squash, peeled, seeded, and cubed (4 cups)

½ teaspoon fine sea salt (divided)

½ teaspoon freshly ground black pepper (divided)

3 tablespoons extra-virgin olive oil (divided)

1 medium onion, diced

2 tablespoons grated peeled fresh ginger

2 tablespoons grated peeled fresh turmeric

2 tablespoons finely chopped garlic

1 teaspoon ground cumin

½ teaspoon ground cinnamon

¼ teaspoon ground coriander

¼ teaspoon red pepper flakes

1 (15-ounce) can chickpeas, rinsed and drained

1 large or 2 small zucchini, cut into chunks

8 dried apricots, thinly sliced

3 cups low-sodium vegetable broth

¼ cup chopped fresh flat-leaf parsley

¼ cup chopped fresh cilantro

In a medium bowl, toss the squash cubes with ¼ teaspoon each salt and pepper. In a large skillet with a lid, heat 2 tablespoons of the oil over medium-high heat. Add the squash and cook until browned on all sides, avoiding moving the pieces around except to flip, 4 to 5 minutes total. Transfer the squash to a bowl and reserve.

Add the remaining 1 tablespoon oil to the skillet, then add the onion and cook, stirring, until softened and translucent, 6 to 7 minutes. Add the ginger, turmeric, garlic, cumin, cinnamon, coriander, red pepper flakes, the remaining ¼ teaspoon salt, and the remaining ¼ teaspoon pepper and cook, stirring, until the spices are fragrant, about 2 minutes.

Return the squash to the pan and add the chickpeas, zucchini, apricots, and broth.

Bring to a boil, reduce the heat, cover, and simmer until the liquid thickens and the squash can be easily pierced with a fork but is not mushy, 12 to 15 minutes. Stir in the parsley and cilantro and serve.

Veggie Mains

Smoky
MILLET-VEGETABLE PAELLA

I'VE ALWAYS LOVED THE ONE-POT-MEAL attributes of paella—how the rice, aromatics, veggies, and other elements come together to create a whole family feast. But I don't usually eat rice, so this book has forced me to think outside of the one-pot box. Millet to the rescue! This seed is high in antioxidants and is a good source of manganese, magnesium, and phosphorus. To replicate the smokiness of sausage—a typical paella ingredient—while keeping this dish vegetarian, I shake in a healthy lashing of smoked paprika, a dried spice with flavor nuance and antioxidant oomph. The cooked tomatoes in this dish actually contribute more immune-boosting lycopene than raw tomatoes; add to that the green bell peppers' huge helping of vitamin C—200 percent of the daily allowance in one serving!—and this recipe is a winner on every front.

---------------*Serves 6*---------------

2 tablespoons extra-virgin olive oil

1 medium onion, chopped

1 large zucchini, diced

2 large green bell peppers, diced

3 garlic cloves, minced

1½ teaspoons smoked paprika

1 teaspoon fine sea salt

¼ teaspoon freshly ground black pepper

3 cups cooked millet (see page 33 and Tip)

2 cups diced tomatoes or 1 (14-ounce) can diced tomatoes with juice

1½ cups vegetable broth

Pinch of saffron

1 cup frozen green peas

¼ cup chopped fresh flat-leaf parsley

Heat the oil in a large skillet over medium-high heat. Add the onion and cook, stirring, until translucent, 7 to 8 minutes. Add the zucchini, bell peppers, garlic, smoked paprika, salt, and pepper and cook, stirring, for about 2 minutes.

Add the millet, tomatoes, broth, and saffron and bring to a boil. Reduce the heat, cover, and simmer until the millet absorbs most of the liquid, 18 to 20 minutes, adding the peas during the last 2 minutes of cooking. Stir in the parsley and serve.

TIP If you can, look for millet labeled hulled (versus pearled); hulled is healthier.

MUNG BEAN DAL
with Mustard Greens and Millet

ONCE IN A WHILE, MY KIDS crave Indian food, and I whip up a pot of this fragrant, delicious vegetarian bean dish. Dal is usually made with lentils, which are high in carbohydrates, which I avoid, but the term is a catchall for a delicately spiced soup-stew based on split pulses or beans. Soaking the mung beans before using makes them easier on the tummy, and they're known to be a friendly source of nutrition for anti-Candida eaters like me. I particularly like mung beans because they contain a healthy dose of protein, fiber, and folate.

Serves 4 to 6

For the dal

1 cup mung beans, soaked for at least 8 hours and up to 24, rinsed, and drained

4½ cups water (divided), plus more if needed

1½ teaspoons fine sea salt (divided)

2 tablespoons coconut oil (see page 23)

1 teaspoon mustard seeds

½ teaspoon cumin seeds

3 cardamom pods

1 tablespoon chopped peeled fresh ginger

1 tablespoon grated peeled fresh turmeric or ½ teaspoon ground

4 garlic cloves, minced

1 jalapeño, seeded (optional) and chopped

For the mustard greens and millet

3 cups cooked millet (see page 33), preferably hot

1 cup thinly sliced mustard greens

1 tablespoon coconut oil

½ teaspoon fine sea salt

¼ teaspoon freshly ground black pepper

Make the dal: In a 3- or 4-quart saucepan, bring the mung beans, 2 cups of the water, and 1 teaspoon of the salt to a boil. Cover, reduce the heat, and simmer until most of the liquid is absorbed and the beans are soft, 10 to 20 minutes (depending on how long you've soaked the beans). Drain, transfer to a bowl, and set aside.

To the same saucepan, add the coconut oil and heat over medium-high heat. Add the mustard seeds, cumin seeds, and cardamom pods and cook until the seeds begin to pop, about 1 minute. Add the ginger, turmeric, garlic, and jalapeño and cook, stirring, until fragrant, 1 to 2 minutes. Return the mung beans to the pan and add the remaining 2½ cups water and the remaining ½ teaspoon salt. Bring to a boil, reduce the heat, and simmer until some of the liquid is absorbed but the dal is still a bit loose, 8 to 10 minutes. (For a looser dal, add an additional ½ to 1 cup water, if desired. The dal will continue to absorb water as it cools.)

Make the mustard greens and millet: In a serving bowl, toss the millet with the greens, oil, salt, and pepper. Serve with the dal.

fish, poultry, and beef

There's no doubt about it—protein is an easy thing to center a dinner around. But unlike the main courses of my past, my recipes that contain an animal protein are now produce-packed, often using the meat as an accent or an equal participant with a bounty of vegetables, herbs, and spices. I almost never serve beef, but I occasionally put some grass-fed bison on the table. When it comes to fish, I seek out choices that respect sustainability. Chicken, of course, must be organic under all circumstances. If possible, I like to know the farmer personally—or at least get a reference from a friend in the know.

My decision to include animal protein in my diet was influenced by Terry Wahls, MD, in her book *Minding My Mitochondria: How I Overcame Secondary Progressive Multiple Sclerosis (MS) and Got Out of My Wheelchair.* Though some aspects of Dr. Wahls' regime don't dovetail with mine, her practice of eating high-quality protein as a path to mitochondrial health resonated with me and my MS journey. Healthy mitochondria (found in every cell) generate energy and enable the storage of vital compounds our body needs, specifically for functions like muscle contraction, brain agility, and tissue repair and regeneration—all of which are compromised when MS is in the picture. So while you won't find me carving roast beef on a daily basis, meat is definitely a part of my diet.

the recipes

POACHED CHICKEN ASIAN "WALDORF" SALAD

IF YOU'RE LOOKING FOR NEW ways to prepare chicken, this may just excite you. Poaching imparts flavor while maintaining moisture. I add lemongrass and lime to the poaching liquid, yielding juicy meat with a mildly Southeast Asian flavor profile. It may sound funny to call this a Waldorf salad, but the walnuts and apple are a signature of the original, mayonnaise-cloaked version.

———————Serves 4 to 6———————

For the poached chicken

1½ pounds boneless, skinless chicken breasts

1 sprig fresh cilantro

1 scallion, bruised with the flat of a knife

3 garlic cloves, peeled and smashed

1 fresh lemongrass stalk, cut into 2-inch pieces, smashed with the flat of a knife

1-inch strips zest from ½ lime

For the dressing

⅓ cup safflower oil

¼ cup coconut aminos (see page 26)

3 tablespoons fresh lime juice

1½ teaspoons finely minced peeled fresh ginger

1½ tablespoons very finely minced fresh lemongrass (pale white parts only)

1 teaspoon coconut palm sugar or nectar (see page 29)

½ teaspoon sea salt

For the salad

1 small head Napa cabbage, thinly sliced (8 cups)

3 cups snow peas, trimmed and thinly sliced

1 cup finely chopped kale

1 medium green or red apple, cut into matchsticks

2 scallions, thinly sliced

½ cup packed fresh cilantro

1 red hot chile, seeded (optional) and thinly sliced

½ cup walnuts, soaked and dehydrated (see page 32), chopped

Make the poached chicken: Place all of the ingredients in a high-sided 10-inch skillet with a lid. Cover the chicken with cold water by 1 inch. Bring to a boil, immediately reduce the heat to a simmer, cover, and simmer until the chicken is just cooked through, 20 to 22 minutes. Remove the chicken from the liquid; discard the liquid. Let the chicken cool completely. Using your hands, shred the chicken into strips.

Make the dressing: In a large salad bowl, whisk together all of the ingredients.

Make the salad: Add the chicken, cabbage, snow peas, kale, apple, scallions, cilantro, and chili to the dressing. Toss, top with the walnuts, and serve.

CEVICHE
in a Snap

CEVICHE IS ONE OF THOSE DISHES where Paleo meets raw at the intersection of delicious. An ideal combination of protein, herbs, and citrus, this recipe comes together with ease and always feels fancy. I call for a shallot, but in a pinch, a couple of scallions would do you just fine.

Serves 6

2 pounds very fresh fish fillets, such as halibut or sea bass, rinsed and patted dry

1½ cups fresh lime juice

½ cup fresh lemon juice

½ red onion, finely chopped

1 large shallot, finely chopped

1 large tomato, chopped

1 large jalapeño, seeded and finely chopped

2 garlic cloves, finely chopped

½ cup grated fresh coconut

Pinch of cayenne pepper

Fine sea salt and freshly ground black pepper

1 avocado, pitted, peeled, and chopped

¼ cup chopped fresh cilantro

2 teaspoons chopped fresh oregano

In a large bowl, toss the fish gently with the lime juice, lemon juice, onion, shallot, tomato, jalapeño, garlic, coconut, cayenne, and salt and pepper to taste. Cover and refrigerate, stirring once, until the fish is slightly opaque, 1 to 2 hours. Gently fold in the avocado, cilantro, and oregano and serve immediately. The ceviche can be refrigerated but should be eaten within 24 hours.

Fish, Poultry, and Beef

SALMON, AVOCADO, AND SHAVED RADISH SASHIMI

IF YOU BUY SUSHI-GRADE SALMON and have a really sharp knife, you can make your family a killer sashimi dinner at a fraction of the cost you'd pay at a restaurant. Lush salmon, rich avocados, sharp radishes: You can't go wrong! The coconut aminos and lime add a tart splash at the end. Go ahead and add a dash of toasted sesame oil if you like, though the dish is so rich on its own, you won't miss it.

—————————Serves 4—————————

½ pound wild, skinless sushi-grade salmon, rinsed, patted dry, pin bones removed, and very thinly sliced

1 firm, ripe avocado, pitted, peeled, and sliced into very thin wedges

4 radishes, very thinly sliced

1 tablespoon coconut aminos (see page 26)

Juice from ½ fresh lime

Microgreens, for garnish

Arrange the salmon, avocado, and radishes on a plate in a pretty pattern. Drizzle with the coconut aminos and the lime juice. Garnish with the microgreens and serve.

CHARD-WRAPPED MAHIMAHI
with Tomatoes and Herbs

THIS DINNER IS DEAD SIMPLE. The fresh chard leaves encase the fish, ensuring that it stays extra-moist even after cooking. The dish can easily be doubled or even tripled for a crowd. Mahimahi is a sustainable seafood choice; ask your fishmonger for "U.S. troll/pole caught," which refers to the fish's American origins, as well as the way it's fished.

Serves 4

1 bunch Swiss chard (8 large leaves), trimmed, leaves separated from stalks

5 tablespoons plus 1 teaspoon extra-virgin olive oil (divided), plus more for drizzling

¼ cup chopped fresh chives (divided), plus more for garnish

2 tablespoons chopped fresh oregano (divided), plus more for garnish

2 tablespoons chopped fresh thyme (divided), plus more for garnish

6 garlic cloves, minced (divided)

1 lemon, finely zested and halved

1½ teaspoons fine sea salt (divided)

½ teaspoon freshly ground black pepper (divided)

4 (6-ounce) skinless mahimahi fillets, rinsed and patted dry

1 (28-ounce) can diced tomatoes, drained of most juice

Preheat the oven to 425°F.

Finely chop the chard stalks and reserve. In a small bowl, combine ¼ cup of the oil, 2 tablespoons of the chives, 1 tablespoon each of the oregano and thyme, half the garlic, the lemon zest, ¾ teaspoon of the salt, and ¼ teaspoon of the pepper. Rub the oil-spice mixture all over the fish fillets and wrap each one in chard leaves, using 2 leaves per fillet if necessary. Place the wrapped fish in a 9-by-13-inch baking dish.

Thinly slice any remaining chard leaves and combine in a large bowl with the reserved chard stalks, the tomatoes, and the remaining 1 tablespoon plus 1 teaspoon oil, the 2 tablespoons chives, 1 tablespoon oregano, 1 tablespoon thyme, garlic, ¾ teaspoon salt, and ¼ teaspoon pepper. Pour the tomato mixture over the fish and squeeze the juice from the 2 lemon halves over the dish.

Bake until the tomato mixture bubbles, 23 to 25 minutes. Divide the fish among four plates, spooning the tomato mixture over the top of each fillet. Garnish with additional chives, oregano, and thyme, drizzle with oil, and serve.

TIP Mahimahi is also known as dolphinfish, but don't worry—it has nothing to do with Flipper.

Jerk-Rubbed
SALMON

MY KIDS' RELATIONSHIP WITH fresh fish is mixed: Sometimes they like it; sometimes they turn up their noses and ask for chicken. That's why I did a double take when my son, Owen, ate an entire plate of this salmon dish, then asked for a second helping. The spice blend is loosely inspired by jerk seasoning but is mellowed to take the superspicy edge off.

——————Serves 5 or 6 ——————

1 teaspoon chili powder

½ teaspoon onion powder

½ teaspoon garlic powder

½ teaspoon paprika

½ teaspoon ground cumin

¼ teaspoon ground ginger

¼ teaspoon fine sea salt

¼ teaspoon freshly ground black pepper

Dash of cayenne pepper

1 (1¾- to 2-pound) side wild salmon, skin on, pin bones removed, rinsed and patted dry

1 tablespoon extra-virgin olive oil

Preheat the oven to 400°F. Line a baking sheet with parchment paper.

In a small bowl, combine the chili powder, onion powder, garlic powder, paprika, cumin, ginger, salt, pepper, and cayenne pepper. Place the salmon skin side down on the baking sheet. Brush the salmon with the oil, then sprinkle the spice blend evenly over the salmon.

Bake until the fish is cooked to the desired doneness, about 15 minutes for medium-rare and 17 to 18 minutes for well done. Serve immediately.

TIPS Much of the omega-3 in salmon is concentrated in the skin. At the very least, bake the fish with the skin on, then slide the flesh off the skin when it's done. If you like, you can then loosen the crisped skin from the parchment and divide it among the willing recipients—it's crunchy, like a potato chip from the sea. My dogs also love it!

Triple or quadruple the spice blend and store it in an airtight container for up to a month. Use it on all kinds of fish, chicken, or beef.

Tahini
BAKED COD

CLOAKING SNOWY WHITE COD in rich tahini sauce creates a divine dinner dish in minutes, one your kids can help put together, too. Paired with a salad, it's a healthy, simple meal.

Serves 4

4 (6-ounce) cod fillets, rinsed, patted dry

Fine sea salt and freshly ground black pepper

1 cup Green-E Tahini (page 95)

4 cups pea tendrils or other microgreens (optional)

Chopped fresh flat-leaf parsley and scallions, for garnish

Preheat the oven to 425°F. Line a baking sheet with parchment paper.

Season the cod fillets with salt and pepper to taste and arrange on the baking sheet. Coat the top of each fillet with ¼ cup of the Green-E Tahini. Bake until the fish is cooked through and flaky, about 12 minutes (if desired, broil the fish for about 1 minute at the end to slightly brown the top). Arrange the pea tendrils on a serving platter and top with the fish. Garnish with the parsley and scallions and serve.

Maple-Walnut
"BAKLAVA" SALMON

WHEN I'M HAVING GUESTS OVER FOR DINNER, I turn to this salmon again and again. It's good straight out of the oven and great at room temperature—any way you slice it, it's a crowd-pleaser. Riffing on the flavors of the classic Turkish dessert, the recipe quick-changes the flavor accents from sweet to savory. The key here is to splurge on the very best salmon you can find. Ask your fishmonger for wild salmon if it's in season; it's preferable to farmed for many reasons. The taste is clean, pure, and lush; the flesh is firm, yet supple. Most notably, studies have shown that wild salmon contains more of the omega-3s your body needs. Add to that some healthy walnuts, maple syrup, and a sprinkle of flax meal, and this is as much a recipe for health as for flavor.

—————————*Serves 4 to 6*—————————

1 (2½-pound) side wild salmon, skin on, pin bones removed, rinsed and patted dry

Fine sea salt and freshly ground black pepper

⅓ cup Grainy Mustard (page 104)

2 tablespoons pure maple syrup

½ cup walnuts, soaked and dehydrated (see page 32), finely chopped

¼ cup chopped fresh flat-leaf parsley, plus more for garnish

2 tablespoons flax meal

Preheat the oven to 400°F. Line a roasting pan with parchment paper.

Place the salmon on the pan and season generously with salt and pepper.

In a small bowl, whisk together the mustard, maple syrup, and pepper to taste. In another bowl, toss the walnuts, parsley, and flax meal. Spread the mustard mixture evenly on the salmon, then pat the walnut mixture on top of the mustard.

Bake until the salmon is just cooked through, 17 to 18 minutes (bake for 3 to 4 minutes more for well done). Garnish with parsley and serve.

NORI ROLLS

LOW-CARB, WRAPPY, SANDWICHY, BURRITO-LIKE STUFF is a favorite in my house, and these wraps fit the bill. Not only is nori—paper-like square sheets of seaweed—high in protein, but it's also loaded with omega-3s, vitamin C, and vitamin B_2. Set out the nori sheets (or lettuce leaves) and all of the other ingredients on a pretty platter, and let family and friends build their own creations. Serve it with my killer Carrot-Ginger Dipping Sauce (page 105).

———————Serves a crowd———————

Whole nori (seaweed) sheets or whole red leaf or butter lettuce leaves

Carrots, peeled and shredded

Cucumbers, halved lengthwise, peeled, seeded, and cut into ¼-inch-thick slices

Daikon radishes, peeled and shredded

Red or orange bell peppers, cut into thin strips

Spinach or Swiss chard leaves, chopped

Cooked boneless, skinless chicken breasts, cut into strips

Cooked salmon fillet, flaked

Avocado wedges

Carrot-Ginger Dipping Sauce (page 105)

Arrange all of the ingredients except the dipping sauce on a platter.

To assemble each roll, place a nori sheet (or lettuce leaf) on a plate.

Layer your choice of ingredients 4 inches from the edge of a nori sheet in a 2-inch-wide strip, leaving room around the edges. Lightly moisten the edges of the nori sheet with water, then pull one edge over the filling, pressing down and tucking it slightly under the filling. Roll into a log, moistening the seam with water to make it stick. Using a serrated knife, cut the roll on the bias into 2 pieces.

Serve with the Carrot-Ginger Dipping Sauce.

Za'atar and Lemon
GRILLED CHICKEN

SPICE BLEND? CHECK. FRESH LEMON? Check. Great dinner? Done. The exotic and the familiar meet here, in a lickety-split dish that tastes like it spent hours marinating. If you have the time to go outside and grill, that little bit of smoke adds something special here, but an indoor griddle or grill pan works fine. When I need to coat a pan with cooking spray, I use only organic olive oil or coconut varieties. I match the spray to the type of cuisine I'm cooking, favoring coconut oil for Asian- or Indian-inspired dishes and olive oil for more Mediterranean-style food.

——————Serves 4 to 6——————

1 lemon, halved; cut 1 half into 4 to 6 wedges; finely zest and juice the other half

¼ cup za'atar (see page 28)

2 tablespoons extra-virgin olive oil

3 garlic cloves, minced

½ teaspoon fine sea salt

¼ teaspoon freshly ground black pepper

1½ pounds chicken cutlets (see Tip)

Olive oil cooking spray

In a medium bowl, whisk the lemon zest and juice with the za'atar, oil, garlic, salt, and pepper until incorporated. Add the chicken to the bowl and toss to coat.

Heat a grill pan or griddle over medium-high heat, then coat with cooking spray. Grill the chicken and lemon wedges until grill marks form, about 3 minutes. Flip and grill until the chicken is fully cooked, 1 to 2 minutes. Serve the chicken with the grilled lemon wedges.

TIP If you can't find chicken cutlets, make your own: Using a sharp knife held parallel to your work surface, carefully slice a boneless, skinless chicken breast horizontally into 2 or 3 pieces of generally equal thickness—but don't worry, the math police won't be coming by with a ruler to check the accuracy of your work.

SINGLE-SKILLET CHICKEN
Puttanesca

BASED ON THE ITALIAN WORD for a less-than-virtuous woman, *puttanesca* to me means all kinds of salty, yummy things gathered together in one skillet. Ordinarily used as a tomato-rich sauce for pasta, this tomato-less version gets lightened up with the addition of more veggies—and is de-carbed by swapping in chicken for noodles. The leeks and garlic provide the benefits of alliums; the olives and capers contain antioxidants; and the roasted red peppers pack vitamin C power.

Serves 6

¼ cup extra-virgin olive oil (divided)

2 pounds chicken cutlets (see Tip, page 199)

Fine sea salt and freshly ground black pepper

1 teaspoon salt-free Italian seasoning

2 large leeks, white and pale green parts only, thoroughly rinsed and thinly sliced into rounds

6 garlic cloves, thinly sliced

1½ cups low-sodium chicken broth

1 (16-ounce) jar fire-roasted red peppers, rinsed, drained, and sliced

1 (14-ounce) can water-packed artichoke hearts, drained and quartered

½ cup sliced pitted green olives

2 tablespoons capers, drained but not rinsed

¼ cup chopped fresh flat-leaf parsley, for garnish

In a large skillet with a lid, heat 2 tablespoons of the oil over medium-high heat. Season the chicken with salt and pepper to taste and the Italian seasoning. Add the chicken to the skillet and brown until golden, about 2 minutes per side. Remove the chicken to a plate and reserve.

Add the remaining 2 tablespoons oil to the juices in the skillet, add the leeks, and cook, stirring, until softened, 3 to 4 minutes. Add the garlic and cook for about 1 minute. Add the broth and cook, scraping the bottom of the skillet to incorporate any browned bits, until the liquid is slightly reduced, 2 to 3 minutes. Stir in the peppers, artichokes, olives, and capers.

Return the chicken to the skillet, reduce the heat to low, cover, and simmer until the flavors are blended, about 10 minutes. Sprinkle with pepper to taste, garnish with the parsley, and serve.

All-Time-Favorite
CHICKEN TENDERS

THESE ARE THINGS THAT HAPPEN regularly in my house: 1) One of my kids forgets the lunch that I lovingly prepared at home. 2) I race to school to deliver it so the kid doesn't resort to eating someone's Lunchables. 3) That lunch contains these chicken tenders, which I make about as often as the sun shines in Boulder (which is to say, almost all the time). By replacing the standard flour with almond flour and flax meal, frying in coconut oil, and adding a ton of great herbs and spices, I've turned a ho-hum standard into one of my go-to dishes. These tenders are good hot, they're good cold—they're just plain good.

————Serves 6————

1 cup almond flour or almond meal (see Tip, page 260)

¾ cup flax meal

⅓ cup salt-free Italian seasoning

¾ teaspoon fine sea salt

½ teaspoon red pepper flakes

½ teaspoon paprika

¼ teaspoon freshly ground black pepper

Pinch of cayenne pepper

2 large eggs, lightly beaten

⅓ cup Raw-mond Milk (page 35) or other unsweetened almond milk

2 pounds boneless, skinless chicken breasts, cut into thin strips

About ½ cup coconut oil (see page 23)

Lemon wedges for serving

Preheat the oven to 350°F. Set a rack on top of a baking sheet.

In a wide, shallow bowl, combine the almond flour, flax meal, Italian seasoning, salt, red pepper flakes, paprika, pepper, and cayenne pepper. In a separate shallow bowl, whisk together the eggs and almond milk. A few at a time, dip the chicken strips first in the egg mixture, then into the flour mixture.

In a large skillet, heat 2 tablespoons of the coconut oil over medium-high heat. Fry the chicken tenders in batches until golden brown, 2 to 3 minutes per side, adding more coconut oil, as needed. Set the browned chicken tenders on the rack.

When all the tenders are browned, finish in the oven until cooked through, about 4 minutes. Serve hot or at room temperature.

TIP Italian Seasoning
A combination of dried oregano, thyme, basil, parsley, marjoram, and other green goodness, Italian seasoning adds great flavor with every shake and provides a healthy shot of antioxidants. Seek out a sodium-free version.

Coconut and Herb Grilled
CHICKEN BREASTS

AMONG MY KITCHEN'S GREATEST HITS, this chicken—fragrant with loads of fresh herbs and tropical coconut milk—makes an appearance at least once a week in Leidich Land. I love it because it feels both highly exotic and extremely homey at the same time. Most of the herbs are permanent residents in my vegetable drawer, but the lemongrass lures taste buds to Southeast Asia, a region whose flavors I turn to often. Rather than scraping off the extra herbs after marinating, leave as many of them clinging to the chicken as possible; that way, when you grill the chicken, the little bits get charred and caramelized.

———————*Serves 4 to 6*———————

¾ cup canned coconut milk

1 cup finely chopped fresh cilantro

1 fresh lemongrass stalk, outer layers removed and discarded, tender inner portion very thinly sliced (about 1 tablespoon)

¼ cup finely chopped fresh basil

2 small Thai bird chilies or jalapeños or 1 medium serrano chili, seeded and finely chopped

2 scallions, very thinly sliced, plus more for garnish

4 garlic cloves, finely minced

2 teaspoons finely grated peeled fresh ginger

2 teaspoons coconut palm sugar (see page 29)

1 teaspoon fine sea salt

¾ teaspoon ground coriander

½ teaspoon freshly ground black pepper

Finely grated zest and juice of 1 lime

12 chicken cutlets (2¼ to 2½ pounds; see Tip page 199)

Coconut oil cooking spray

Lime wedges for serving

In a large bowl, combine all of the ingredients except the chicken cutlets, cooking spray, and lime wedges. Add the chicken cutlets and turn to coat completely. Cover and refrigerate for at least 2 hours and up to 12 hours.

Heat a griddle or grill pan over medium-high heat and coat with cooking spray. Working in batches, remove the chicken from the marinade, letting as many herbs as possible cling to the surface. Cook the chicken until browned and cooked through, 2 to 3 minutes per side. Garnish the chicken with sliced scallions and serve with the lime wedges.

Fish, Poultry, and Beef

Herb-Roasted
TURKEY BREAST

THIS JUICY, HERBY TURKEY BREAST can be the centerpiece of a nice dinner for company or a great source of protein for a week's worth of school lunches and snacks. The secret is to tent the turkey with parchment for the first part of roasting, which keeps the meat nice and moist.

Serve this with Goldenberry and Caramelized Onion Chelish (page 106), Twice-Baked Smashed Sweet Potatoes (page 241), and Shaved Brussels Sprout Salad with Lemony Lucuma Dressing (page 158).

Serves 6

2 tablespoons extra-virgin olive oil

2 garlic cloves, minced

1 tablespoon chopped fresh thyme or 1½ teaspoons dried

1 tablespoon chopped fresh oregano or 1½ teaspoons dried

1 teaspoon finely chopped fresh rosemary or ½ teaspoon dried

2 teaspoons ground dried eleuthero (see page 26)

1 teaspoon finely grated lemon zest

½ teaspoon fine sea salt

¼ teaspoon freshly ground black pepper

¼ teaspoon red pepper flakes

1 (2½- to 3-pound) bone-in, skin-on turkey breast half

Preheat the oven to 350°F.

In a small bowl, combine the oil, garlic, thyme, oregano, rosemary, eleuthero, lemon zest, salt, pepper, and red pepper flakes to make a thick paste. Rub the paste all over the turkey breast and set it in a 9-by-13-inch baking dish. Tent loosely with parchment paper and roast for 1 hour. Remove the parchment tent and continue to roast until the turkey's internal temperature reaches 165°F on a meat thermometer inserted into the thickest part of the breast and the juices run clear, 35 to 40 minutes.

Remove the turkey from the oven and let it rest for 10 minutes, then carefully pour the pan juices into a gravy boat. Slice the turkey across the grain and serve with the pan juices.

Stress-Busting
TURKEY MEATBALLS

FLAX MEAL BINDS THESE BABIES together the way eggs might (sub in an egg for the flaxseeds if you don't have any). In small amounts, eleuthero and ashwagandha help the body regulate stress and maintain balance (happy adrenals make for a happy mama). In these amounts, they don't add any discernible taste but improve my health in ways I can feel. (See photo, pages 208–209.)

Serves 4

1 pound ground turkey

1 cup finely chopped baby spinach

1 small carrot, peeled and finely shredded

1 shallot, minced

5 garlic cloves, minced

1 teaspoon fine sea salt

¼ teaspoon freshly ground black pepper

2 tablespoons flax meal

2 teaspoons salt-free Italian seasoning

¼ cup chopped fresh flat-leaf parsley

1½ teaspoons dried (not ground) eleuthero (see page 26)

½ teaspoon ashwagandha (see page 25)

2 tablespoons extra-virgin olive oil

4 cups Fresh Tomato Sauce (page 165) or good-quality store-bought marinara sauce

Cooked brown rice noodles or other organic, gluten-free noodles, for serving

In a large bowl, combine the turkey, spinach, carrot, shallot, garlic, salt, pepper, flax meal, Italian seasoning, parsley, eleuthero, and ashwagandha and mix well. Form into walnut-sized balls.

In a large skillet, heat the oil over medium-high heat. Working in batches, brown the meatballs until golden, turning occasionally, 5 to 6 minutes total.

In a 4-quart saucepan, heat the tomato sauce until simmering, then gently lower the meatballs into the sauce. Simmer until the meatballs absorb some of the sauce and soften, 50 to 60 minutes. Serve over the noodles.

Stress-Busting Turkey Meatballs (page 207)

INDIAN TURKEY BURGERS
with Cucumber "Raita"

YOGURT, SCHMOGURT! THE CREAMY, DAIRY-FREE RAITA I use to sauce these spicy, highly seasoned turkey burgers is made with little more than macadamia nuts, water, and salt, with chopped cucumbers stirred in for crunch.

—Makes 10 burgers; serves 4 to 6—

For the cucumber raita

1 cup macadamia nuts, soaked and dehydrated (see page 32)

1 cup water

Finely grated zest and juice of 1 lime

1 teaspoon fine sea salt

1 small Persian cucumber or ¼ English cucumber, peeled, seeded, and finely diced

For the burgers

1½ pounds ground turkey breast

4 scallions, thinly sliced

½ cup finely chopped celery

½ Granny Smith apple, finely diced

1 tablespoon grated peeled fresh turmeric

1 tablespoon freshly grated peeled fresh ginger

1 tablespoon minced garlic

1 teaspoon curry powder

1 small jalapeño, seeded (optional) and finely chopped

Finely grated zest and juice of 1 lime

½ cup chopped fresh flat-leaf parsley

1 teaspoon fine sea salt

1 teaspoon freshly ground black pepper

½ teaspoon ground cinnamon

½ teaspoon ground cumin

¼ teaspoon ground coriander

Melted coconut oil (see page 23), for grilling

Make the cucumber raita: In a blender, combine the macadamia nuts, water, lime zest, cucumber, lime juice, and salt and blend until smooth. Transfer to a small bowl and stir in the cucumber.

Make the burgers: Combine all of the ingredients except the coconut oil and form the mixture into 10 patties, each 1 inch thick and 4 inches in diameter.

Heat a griddle or grill pan over medium-high heat and brush with coconut oil. Grill the burgers until cooked through, 3 to 4 minutes per side, and serve with the raita.

TIP The uncooked burger patties can be individually frozen, sealed tightly in parchment paper packets, for 1 month.

BISON BURGERS

I PREFER THE LEAN and mineral-rich taste of bison to the heaviness of beef. Plus, there's only so much salad my kids will eat, and animal protein delivers a bundle of nutrients and an energy jolt. The chopped chard helps keep the meat moist.

————Serves 6————

1½ pounds ground bison

3 large Swiss chard leaves, finely chopped

½ cup finely minced onion

2 tablespoons coconut aminos (see page 26)

2 garlic cloves, minced

½ teaspoon fine sea salt

¼ teaspoon freshly ground black pepper

Olive oil cooking spray

6 raw collard green leaf halves (ribs removed), for serving

In a medium bowl, combine the bison, chard, onion, coconut aminos, garlic, salt, and pepper and gently mix until incorporated. Form the mixture into 6 patties, each 1 inch thick and 4 inches in diameter.

Heat a grill, grill pan, or griddle over medium-high heat and coat with cooking spray.

Grill the burgers until the exterior is charred and the interior is cooked to your liking, 4 to 5 minutes per side. Wrap with the collard leaves and serve.

Fish, Poultry, and Beef

BOK CHOY, SIX-ONION, AND BISON STIR-FRY

BISON HAS A REP FOR BEING TOUGHER than beef, but I get great results by seasoning the meat generously and making sure I don't overcook it. The bison is the perfect foil for six—count 'em—kinds of healthy alliums.

————Serves 4————

1 pound boneless, grass-fed bison rib-eye steak, thinly sliced

1 tablespoon chili powder

2 garlic cloves, minced

1 teaspoon fine sea salt (divided)

¼ teaspoon red pepper flakes

3 tablespoons extra-virgin olive oil (divided)

1 small sweet onion, thinly sliced

1 leek, white and light green parts, well rinsed and thinly sliced

½ small red onion, thinly sliced

1 large shallot, minced

3 scallions, cut into 2-inch lengths

1 pound baby bok choy, thinly sliced, paler stems and leafier green parts separated

1 red bell pepper, chopped

In a medium bowl, toss the bison slices, chili powder, garlic, ½ teaspoon of the salt, and the red pepper flakes.

In a very large (at least 12-inch) skillet, heat 1 tablespoon of the oil over medium-high heat. Add the bison in a single layer and cook, turning once, until browned and just cooked through, 1 to 2 minutes per side. Remove the meat to a bowl and reserve.

Add the remaining 2 tablespoons oil to the skillet, then add the sweet onion, leek, red onion, shallot, and scallions and cook, stirring occasionally, until the onions are browned and softened, 7 to 8 minutes. Add the bok choy stems and cook, stirring, until crisp-tender, 1 to 2 minutes.

Add the reserved bison and the remaining ½ teaspoon salt and cook, stirring, until warmed through, 1 to 2 minutes. Remove from the heat and stir in the bok choy greens and bell pepper. Serve immediately.

CHAPTER 8

veggie sides and savory snacks

For me, these vegetable dishes can be as much a midafternoon pick-me-up as a meal accompaniment. I find myself turning to them again and again, and they never disappoint me. Often I use a base vegetable ingredient as the foil for healthy add-ons that amp up the nutrition, giving me one more reason to get excited about making them.

the recipes

ROASTY, TOASTY BRUSSELS SPROUTS
with Flaxseeds

LOOKING LIKE TINY CABBAGES, Brussels sprouts fall into the cruciferous family of vegetables, which are believed to have cancer-reducing properties. They mitigate oxidative stress and reduce the levels of free radicals in the body. The sprouts also contain a healthy dose of omega-3s. Vitamin C and folic acid up the healthy ante. Typically, I grind my flaxseeds, which makes them easier to digest, but when left whole and roasted with the veggies, they give a pleasing crunch.

————Serves 4 to 6————

1½ pounds Brussels sprouts

½ cup garlic cloves, peeled

3 tablespoons extra-virgin olive oil

2 tablespoons whole flaxseeds

½ teaspoon fine sea salt

¼ teaspoon freshly ground black pepper

¼ teaspoon ground turmeric

Preheat the oven to 400°F. Line a baking sheet with parchment paper.

Using a paring knife, trim the sprouts, cut an X into the trimmed bottom of each sprout, and place in a large bowl. Add the remaining ingredients and toss to coat.

Transfer to the baking sheet. Roast, stirring every 10 minutes, until the sprouts are golden and the garlic is tender, about 30 minutes. Serve.

CARAMELIZED CUMIN- AND ORANGE-SCENTED CARROTS
with Walnut Dukkah Seasoning

IF POSSIBLE, SEEK OUT THE gorgeous multicolored, very thin carrots you can find at fancier grocers or the greenmarket. Roasted, their visual appeal matches the natural goodness of the ingredients. The dukkah seasoning, adapted from a classic Egyptian recipe, combines the goodness of seeds, nuts, and antioxidant spices. You'll have some dukkah left over, but I know you'll find oodles of uses for it. A few ideas: Sprinkle it on salads, stir-fries, and grilled fish or chicken.

Serves 4 to 6

2 tablespoons extra-virgin olive oil

Finely grated zest of 1 orange

1 tablespoon fresh orange juice

1 teaspoon ground cumin

2 garlic cloves, minced

¼ teaspoon ground turmeric

¼ teaspoon ashwagandha (see page 25)

¼ teaspoon fine sea salt

⅛ teaspoon freshly ground black pepper

1 pound thin carrots, preferably multicolored, peeled and halved lengthwise

2 tablespoons coconut nectar (see page 29) or pure maple syrup

Walnut Dukkah Seasoning (recipe on opposite page), for sprinkling

Chopped fresh flat-leaf parsley and scallions, for garnish

Preheat the oven to 400°F. Line a baking sheet with parchment paper.

In a large bowl, whisk together the oil, orange zest and juice, cumin, garlic, turmeric, ashwagandha, salt, and pepper. Add the carrots and toss to coat.

Transfer to the baking sheet. Roast for 15 minutes. Turn and drizzle with the coconut nectar and roast until caramelized and crisp-tender, 15 to 20 minutes more.

Arrange on a serving platter, sprinkle with the dukkah seasoning, garnish with parsley and scallions, and serve.

Walnut Dukkah Seasoning

Makes 2 cups

½ cup sesame seeds

3 tablespoons coriander seeds

3 tablespoons cumin seeds

2 tablespoons flaxseeds

1 cup walnuts, soaked and dehydrated (see page 32)

1 teaspoon coconut palm sugar (see page 29)

1 teaspoon flaky sea salt

1 teaspoon freshly ground black pepper

Spread the sesame seeds, coriander seeds, cumin seeds, and flaxseeds on a dehydrator tray lined with a nonstick dehydrator sheet (see page 36) and dehydrate at 118°F until fragrant, 3 to 4 hours.

Grind the dehydrated spices in a spice grinder until fine, then transfer to a food processor. Add the walnuts, coconut palm sugar, salt, and pepper and pulse until the mixture looks like coarse sand, being careful not to overprocess the nuts into a paste, 20 to 25 pulses.

Transfer to an airtight container and store in a cool, dry place for up to 1 month.

ZA'ATAR ROASTED CAULIFLOWER

UNTIL RECENTLY, ZA'ATAR (pronounced zah-*tahr*) wasn't on my kitchen radar, but I was hooked from the minute I tasted the slightly tangy herb blend with roots in the Middle Eastern kitchen. When I did a little more digging, I discovered it was full of good-for-you things like sesame seeds, sumac (which lends za'atar its signature lemony zing and is believed to contain antioxidant properties), oregano, and thyme (more antioxidants!). Sprinkling it on vegetables before roasting is an almost guaranteed way to get even the most finicky kids to hoover down their vegetables. You can swap broccoli in for cauliflower. Use any leftovers (as if!) in salads.

Serves 4 to 6

¼ cup extra-virgin olive oil

2 tablespoons za'atar (see page 28)

½ teaspoon fine sea salt

¼ teaspoon freshly ground black pepper

1 large head cauliflower, core removed, cut into small florets

2 cups Green-E Tahini (page 95)

Preheat the oven to 375°F. Line two baking sheets with parchment paper.

In a large bowl, whisk together the oil, za'atar, salt, and pepper. Add the cauliflower florets and toss to coat.

Divide between the baking sheets. Roast, stirring once midway through, until the cauliflower is soft, golden, and caramelized, 30 to 35 minutes. Spread the tahini on a serving platter, arrange the roasted cauliflower on top, and serve.

Silky
CAULIFLOWER PUREE

HERE, BRASSICA STAR-VEGETABLE CAULIFLOWER—packed with vitamin C, vitamin K, fiber, and folic acid—steps into a creamy puree and turns the standard spud into an also-ran. I didn't tell the kids what this was, and they didn't ask—they were too busy nodding their approval. The blender (use a Vitamix here, if you can) turns the cauliflower supersilky and feather-light—a great side dish for a bison steak or burger.

——————Serves 4 to 6——————

1 medium head cauliflower, cut into small florets, core trimmed and chopped

1 cup Raw-mond Milk (page 35) or other unsweetened almond milk, plus more if necessary

3 tablespoons extra-virgin olive oil, plus more for drizzling

1 teaspoon fine sea salt

¼ teaspoon freshly ground black pepper

Sliced scallion greens, for garnish

Set aside ½ cup of the cauliflower florets. Place the rest of the cauliflower in a steamer basket and steam over simmering water until tender, about 10 minutes. Cool slightly, then transfer to a blender.

Add the almond milk, oil, salt, and pepper to the blender and puree until smooth, about 15 seconds, adding more almond milk by the tablespoonful if necessary. Transfer to a serving bowl and top with the reserved cauliflower florets and the scallions. Drizzle with oil and serve.

RAW CAULIFLOWER AND HEMP "COUSCOUS"

SKIP THE COOKED STUFF and serve this crunchy, sauce-soaking alternative starring a humble head of cauliflower. Take the time to chop the cauliflower into tiny pieces—it makes a real difference here, helping approximate the texture and function of actual couscous. A cruciferous vegetable like its cousin broccoli, cauliflower in its raw state contains glucosinolates, which become cancer-fighting agents when chewed. It's also packed with vitamins C and K, essential for healthy blood and bones. You can serve this with Butternut Squash and Chickpea Tagine (page 177).

Serves 4

1 large head cauliflower, florets only, cut into very tiny dice

¼ cup hemp seeds

¼ cup chopped fresh flat-leaf parsley

¼ cup chopped fresh cilantro

1 tablepoon extra-virgin olive oil

¼ teaspoon fine sea salt

¼ teaspoon freshly ground black pepper

In a large bowl, toss all of the ingredients together. Serve.

SAUTÉED SWISS CHARD
with Goji Berries and Hemp Seeds

SINCE WE'RE A SUPERFOODS-HEAVY HOME, I'm always tweaking classic recipes to bring them in line with the way I like to eat. My version of classic sautéed spinach swaps out the spinach for chard and the currants for tart goji berries and forgoes the pine nuts for a sprinkling of hemp seeds. If you choose to do so, sautéing with coconut oil adds an even nuttier flavor. This dish is also a looker. Though presentation isn't always top of mind for me, the gorgeous goji berries peeking out from among the dark greens make me feel like a food stylist. (See photo, pages 226–227.)

————————*Serves 6*————————

2 tablespoons extra-virgin olive oil or coconut oil (see page 23)

1 large shallot, chopped

3 garlic cloves, minced

2 large bunches rainbow chard, leaves separated from stems, leaves cut into thin ribbons and stems finely chopped

¼ cup dried goji berries

Finely grated zest and juice of 1 lemon (divided)

½ teaspoon fine sea salt

¼ teaspoon freshly ground black pepper

Water, if needed

¼ cup hemp seeds, soaked and dehydrated (see page 32)

In a large skillet or wide-bottomed pot, heat the oil over medium-high heat. Add the shallot and garlic and cook until softened, 2 minutes. Add the chopped chard stems and cook until they begin to soften, 1 to 2 minutes. Working in two additions, add the chard leaves and cook, stirring, until just wilted, 2 to 3 minutes total. Add the goji berries, lemon zest, salt, and pepper and cook until the gojis begin to soften, 1 to 2 minutes, adding water by the tablespoonful if necessary to prevent the greens from sticking and burning. Transfer the chard to a serving platter, drizzle the lemon juice over it, sprinkle with the hemp seeds, and serve.

Composting in the Kitchen

A countertop composter is a permanent fixture in our kitchen. Composting is not institutionalized in every city, but if yours isn't a curbside-composting town, chances are there's a drop-off facility not far from you. In my house, we use the Full Circle Fresh Air Compost Collector, which costs around $30 (not including the bags) and doesn't take up much counter space.

Marinated Collard
Green and Artichoke Heart
ANTIPASTO

THIS IS MY TAKE ON those yummy marinated salads you get from Italian delis. It's adapted from my mother-in-law's recipe and loaded with salty and savory elements. My husband, Greg, could eat a whole bowl of this in one sitting—in fact, I think he has. Traditionally, collards are cooked to within an inch of their life, but at my house, we just slice them up and bathe them in a tangy marinade that keeps their nutrients—vitamin K for blood health, beta carotene for vision, and a bunch of others—intact. Not only are they healthier like this, but I also prefer the way they taste.

————————Serves 4————————

¼ cup unfiltered apple cider vinegar

3 tablespoons extra-virgin olive oil

6 water-packed artichoke
hearts, drained and sliced

¼ cup thinly sliced oil-packed
sun-dried tomatoes

¼ cup thinly sliced scallions

2 garlic cloves, minced

½ teaspoon red pepper flakes

1 teaspoon fine sea salt

½ teaspoon freshly ground black pepper

1 large bunch collard greens,
stalks removed and discarded

¼ cup thinly sliced green or black olives

In a large bowl, whisk together the vinegar and oil. Add the artichokes, sun-dried tomatoes, scallions, garlic, red pepper flakes, salt, and pepper and stir to combine.

A few at a time, stack the collard leaves, roll them into a long, tight cylinder, and slice crosswise into very thin strips. Add the collards and olives to the bowl and toss to incorporate with the rest of the ingredients. Cover and refrigerate for at least 4 hours and up to 12 hours before serving.

Totally Naked
KALE CHIPS

HERE'S A SNACK WORTH HAVING in your arsenal: quick, easy, and power-packed with kale's nutritional goodness. I eat kale chips on their own or add them to anything that needs a bit of crunch. Many kale chips on the market today are loaded with gunk, but we like ours naked, to let the goodness of the kale shine through.

———————*Makes 3 cups chips*———————

1 large bunch dinosaur (lacinato) or curly kale, rinsed and completely dried

1 tablespoon extra-virgin olive oil

¼ teaspoon fine sea salt

Preheat the oven to 350°F. Line two baking sheets with parchment paper.

Separate the kale leaves from the stems, discarding the stems. Tear or cut the kale leaves into large, bite-sized pieces. In a large bowl, toss the kale with the oil and salt, then arrange the leaves in a single layer on the baking sheets. Bake until crisp, about 14 minutes.

To dehydrate: Omit the oil and arrange the kale in a single layer on dehydrator trays lined with nonstick dehydrator sheets (see page 35). Sprinkle with the salt. Dehydrate at 118°F until crisp and dried, flipping once, 6 to 8 hours total.

Meaty Maitake
MUSHROOM FILLING

SINCE I TRY TO FOLLOW a Candida-free diet, mushrooms are a food I avoid (some believe that they promote yeast production and inflammation in the body, especially when eaten in combination with sugary foods). One happy exception is maitake mushrooms, the beautiful frilly specimens you'll find at farmers' markets and nicer supermarkets. Not only are they incredibly tender and meaty, but they're considered by many to be "medicinal" mushrooms that contain immune-boosting properties. This maitake filling passes the kid test—everyone is happy to pile it inside Juicing Crepes (page 83). You can also serve it as a vegetarian filling for any taco or wrap.

—————————————*Serves 4*—————————————

3 tablespoons extra-virgin olive oil

1 large onion, chopped

5 garlic cloves, thinly sliced

1½ pounds maitake mushrooms, trimmed and cut into 1-inch chunks

2 teaspoons chopped fresh thyme

1 teaspoon fine sea salt

¼ teaspoon freshly ground black pepper

In a large skillet, heat the oil over medium-high heat. Add the onion and cook, stirring, until softened and lightly browned around the edges, 9 to 10 minutes. Add the garlic and cook, stirring, for about 1 minute. Add the mushrooms and cook, stirring occasionally, until they soften and release some of their liquid, 4 to 5 minutes. Add the thyme, salt, and pepper and cook for 1 minute. Serve.

Immune-Boosting
ROASTED ONIONS WITH HERBS

WHENEVER YOU HAVE EXTRA ONIONS lying around (which in my house is most of the time), make these sweet, caramelized rounds. If you happen to have Vidalias or some other variety of sweet onion, great—but the plain, old tear-inducing kind works great, too. Roasting obliterates any hint of sharpness, and a sprinkle of eleuthero adds a health benefit. Swap in any fresh herbs you have around, but thyme and onions are a killer combination. Best of all, once you get the onions prepped, they caramelize to perfection all on their own in the hot oven. Though these are great as a side dish, you can also chop them up and add them to soups, salads, and sides for extra impact.

————Serves 4 to 6————

¼ cup extra-virgin olive oil

2 tablespoons chopped fresh thyme

2 tablespoons chopped fresh oregano

1 teaspoon ground dried eleuthero (see page 26)

1½ teaspoons fine sea salt

½ teaspoon freshly ground black pepper

3 large or 5 medium sweet onions (about 2 pounds total), sliced into ¼-inch-thick rounds

Preheat the oven to 400°F. Line two baking sheets with parchment paper.

In a small bowl, combine the oil, thyme, oregano, eleuthero, salt, and pepper. Brush the onion rounds on both sides with the oil mixture and divide between the baking sheets. Cover with parchment and roast until softened, 20 to 25 minutes.

Uncover, reduce the heat to 350°F, and continue to roast until the onions are golden and the undersides are caramelized, 25 to 30 minutes. Serve warm or at room temperature.

Ginger, Garlic, and Coconut
SAUTÉED SPINACH

THIS SPEEDY SIDE DISH HAS A DOUBLE DOSE of coconut: luscious, fragrant oil and crunchy shreds. I know it's supposed to serve four, but I sometimes eat it all by itself for a simple vegetarian lunch. The recipe may seem to call for a large amount of spinach, but it cooks down dramatically.

——————Serves 4——————

3 tablespoons coconut oil (see page 23)

2 tablespoons grated peeled fresh ginger

3 garlic cloves, minced

2 pounds baby spinach

Fine sea salt and freshly ground black pepper

2 tablespoons, unsweetened shredded coconut

In a very large (12-inch) skillet, heat the oil over medium-high heat. Add the ginger and garlic and cook until fragrant, about 15 seconds. In two additions, add the spinach and cook, stirring, until just wilted, 1 to 2 minutes. Season the spinach with salt and pepper to taste. Transfer to a serving bowl, stir in the shredded coconut, and serve.

Crispy
ZUCCHINI CHIPS

AVOCADO OIL HAS A HIGH SMOKE POINT—the temperature at which oil begins to burn—and is great for frying. Here, I shallow-fry zucchini into crispy, wispy chips that are better than potato chips any day. My advice? Double the recipe.

——————Serves 4 to 6——————

2 large zucchini, very thinly sliced with a mandoline slicer or a sharp knife

¼ cup avocado oil or coconut oil (see page 23), plus more as needed

Fine sea salt and freshly ground black pepper

Paprika

Arrange the zucchini slices in a single layer on paper towels and blot away extra moisture.

In a medium skillet, heat the oil over medium-high heat. Working in batches, fry the zucchini until crisp and lightly browned, flipping some chips if necessary, 2 to 3 minutes total.

Drain on a paper-towel-lined plate, season with salt, pepper, and paprika to taste, and serve immediately.

SPINACH BUNDLES
with Sweet-and-Savory Sesame Drizzle

THIS IS ALWAYS THE BEST APPETIZER at sushi restaurants, and once you make it yourself, you'll marvel at how easy it is. If I could keep the whole thing raw, I would, but there's something about the squeaky texture of squishy, just-cooked spinach leaves that approximates the restaurant experience. The four-ingredient drizzle is an exercise in Zen-like simplicity—but has the complexity of days spent in the kitchen.

—————*Makes 10 bundles*—————

3 tablespoons coconut aminos (see page 26) or gluten-free tamari

3 tablespoons raw tahini, store-bought or homemade (page 95)

½ teaspoon coconut palm sugar (see page 29; optional)

½ teaspoon toasted sesame oil

1 pound baby spinach (divided)

2 scallions, thinly sliced

2 tablespoons gomasio (see box) or lightly toasted sesame seeds (divided)

In a small bowl, whisk together the coconut aminos, tahini, coconut palm sugar (if using), and oil and reserve. Finely chop 2 cups of the spinach leaves and reserve.

Bring a large (at least 8-quart) pot of water to a boil. Just as the water comes to a boil, fill a large bowl with water and ice cubes to create an ice water bath. Submerge the remaining spinach in the boiling water and cook, stirring once or twice, until wilted, about 2 minutes. Using a large slotted spoon, remove the spinach from the boiling water and submerge it in the ice water bath until cooled, 1 to 2 minutes. Arrange a large kitchen towel (one you don't mind potentially staining a lovely shade of green) on a work surface near your sink. Remove the spinach from the ice water bath, place it in the center of the towel, and fold the towel over the spinach, securing tightly. Over the sink, twist the ends of the towel toward the spinach-filled center, squeezing as tightly as you can to extract as much water as possible.

What Is Gomasio?
A Japanese seasoning blend, gomasio—available at Asian markets, health food stores, or online—is a savory, nutty combination of sesame seeds (black or white), salt, and sometimes seaweed. It's especially good on Asian food, but I shake it on whatever needs a boost.

Roughly chop the wilted spinach, transfer to a large bowl, and toss with the reserved raw chopped spinach, the scallions, and 4 teaspoons of the gomasio. Pack a 1-inch round cookie cutter with some spinach mixture, then pop it out from the top onto a serving platter (if you don't have the cookie cutter, form with your hands). Repeat with the remaining spinach. Drizzle the dressing on the spinach bundles and garnish with the remaining 2 teaspoons gomasio.

No-Carb
PALEO CRACKERS

I NOW ROTATE THESE NUTTY, crispy crackers into my snacking regime alongside our Two Moms in the Raw Sea Crackers, and I feel liberated because I no longer have to miss out on the crunch of the carb-filled crackers I left behind. My kids love them, finishing them as fast as I can make them. Almonds contribute vitamin E, the egg contributes omega-3, and the mix-ins contribute endless variety. The trick is to roll the crackers as thinly as you can—then roll them more. Finer, sandier almond flour yields a smoother cracker, while almond meal, which sometimes includes larger bits and almond skins, results in a cracker that has a whole-graininess to it.

—————Makes 48 crackers—————

2 cups almond meal or almond flour (see Tip, page 260)

1 large egg

2 tablespoons extra-virgin olive oil

½ teaspoon fine sea salt

Mix-ins (optional)

Italian: 2 tablespoons salt-free Italian seasoning, 1 tablespoon onion flakes

Cinnamon-Sugar: ¼ cup coconut palm sugar (see page 29), 1 teaspoon ground cinnamon

Seeds: 2 tablespoons each black and white sesame seeds, 1 teaspoon cumin seeds

Preheat the oven to 350°F.

Combine the almond meal, egg, oil, and salt in a bowl until moistened. Add the mix-ins of your choice, if desired. Divide the dough in half and form each half into a 4-inch square about 1 inch thick. Roll each square between two sheets of parchment paper until very thin.

Transfer each piece of parchment-covered dough to a baking sheet, peel off the top parchment layer, and cut the dough into 2-by-2-inch squares with a pizza wheel or sharp knife. Bake the crackers until lightly browned on the edges and golden in the center, 10 to 13 minutes depending on thinness. Cool, then separate into crackers and serve. The crackers can be stored in an airtight container for up to 2 weeks.

Flaxy
SWEET POTATER TOTS

MY MOM, MARSHA, TOLD ME about some yummy sweet potato "Tater Tots" she'd had in Florida, then challenged me to re-create them. Sweet potatoes in a tater tot? Heresy! But, as is usually the case, Mom was right. After some tinkering, we came up with these irresistibly crispy little bites, filled with cauliflower and flax meal, that develop a crazy crunch after a fry in heart-healthy olive oil. Just make sure you don't heat the olive oil too high, as it will smoke if overheated. Power-packed with vitamins A and C, these tots are also beta carotene rock stars.

—————Makes 25 tots—————

1 very large sweet potato, peeled and cut into 2-inch chunks

¾ cup very finely minced raw cauliflower florets

1 cup plus 3 tablespoons flax meal (divided)

2 tablespoons nutritional yeast (optional)

2 garlic cloves, minced

1 teaspoon fine sea salt (divided)

⅛ teaspoon freshly ground black pepper

Extra-virgin olive oil, for frying

Place the sweet potato chunks in a steamer basket and steam over simmering water until tender, about 25 minutes. Cool slightly, then mash in a large bowl (you should have about 1½ cups). Add the cauliflower, 3 tablespoons of the flax meal, the nutritional yeast (if using), garlic, ½ teaspoon of the salt, and the pepper and mix well to incorporate.

In a shallow bowl, combine the remaining 1 cup flax meal and the remaining ½ teaspoon salt. Using damp hands, roll the sweet potato mixture, 1 tablespoon at a time, into tater tot–shaped nuggets, about 2 inches long by 1 inch in diameter. Roll each tot in the flax meal until fully coated.

In a large skillet, heat ½ inch oil over medium heat until very hot but not smoking. Working in batches, fry the tots until golden, 1 to 2 minutes per side, adding more oil as necessary and replacing the oil as needed. Drain on a paper-towel-lined plate and serve.

Twice-Baked
SMASHED SWEET POTATOES

I DON'T EAT STARCHY WHITE POTATOES, but these spuds are another story altogether. Enjoyed in moderation, sweet potatoes deliver beta carotene, vitamins A and C, and fiber and have a glycemic index that's way lower than their pale relatives. These "smashed" potatoes are baked in rustic chunks, then compressed to create free-form disks with crispy edges. If you press down hard enough, then bake them long enough, they become almost like thick chips and are suitable for dipping.

——————Serves 4 to 6——————

2 very large sweet potatoes, scrubbed and cut into 2-inch chunks

3 tablespoons extra-virgin olive oil

2 teaspoons chopped fresh rosemary or 1 teaspoon dried

½ teaspoon fine sea salt

¼ teaspoon freshly ground black pepper

Preheat the oven to 400°F. Line two baking sheets with parchment paper.

In a large bowl, toss the potatoes with the oil, rosemary, salt, and pepper. Spread evenly among the baking sheets.

Bake until tender, 35 to 40 minutes. Remove the baking sheet from the oven. Using a potato masher or a large fork, gently smash down the sweet potato chunks (the thinner you smash them, the crispier they will get). Return the potatoes to the oven and bake until the undersides are caramelized, 10 to 15 minutes. Serve.

ROOT-TASTIC LATKES

POTATO LATKES ARE TRADITIONALLY SERVED on Hanukkah, the Jewish festival of lights, and these are a healthier version of the ones my Aunt Susan used to make every year. Without a white potato or any white flour for binding, but with plenty of sweet and savory root vegetables, these lacy-edged rounds are a no-fail way to get your kids to eat their vegetables—and to impress your guests. If you use coconut oil, the pancakes will caramelize and have a nutty flavor; olive oil tends to brown the pancakes a bit more evenly, but they won't be quite as crisp.

————Serves 10 to 12 (makes 32 to 36 latkes)————

2 to 2½ pounds total assorted root and other vegetables, such as parsnips, sweet potatoes, broccoli stems, zucchini, yellow squash, and carrots, trimmed

2 shallots, peeled

4 large eggs

¾ cup almond flour or almond meal (see Tip, page 260) or coconut flour (see page 26)

¼ cup flax meal

1 tablespoon psyllium husks (see page 28)

2 garlic cloves, minced

¼ cup chopped fresh chives

1½ teaspoons fine sea salt

½ teaspoon freshly ground black pepper

Coconut oil (page 23) or extra-virgin olive oil, for frying

Preheat the oven to 225°F.

In a food processor or by hand with a box grater or julienne peeler, shred all of the vegetables and the shallots. Working in batches, place a mound of shredded vegetables in the center of a kitchen towel. Over the sink, squeeze as much excess liquid from the vegetables as possible.

Transfer the vegetables to a large bowl, then add the eggs, almond flour, flax meal, psyllium husks, garlic, chives, salt, and pepper and stir (I use my hands) until the mixture sticks together; let the mixture rest in the bowl for 10 minutes.

In a large skillet, heat ¼ inch oil over medium-high heat. Working in batches, drop about ¼ cup batter into the skillet for each latke, making sure not to overcrowd. Using a spatula, press down on each pile of batter to flatten. Fry until the underside is a deep golden brown with crisped edges, 3 to 4 minutes. Flip and fry until browned on the other side, 2 to 3 minutes. Using a slotted spatula, transfer the latkes to a paper-towel-lined baking sheet and keep warm in the oven. Repeat with the remaining batter, adding more oil to the skillet as needed and replacing the oil completely after the third batch. Serve hot.

Veggie Sides and Savory Snacks

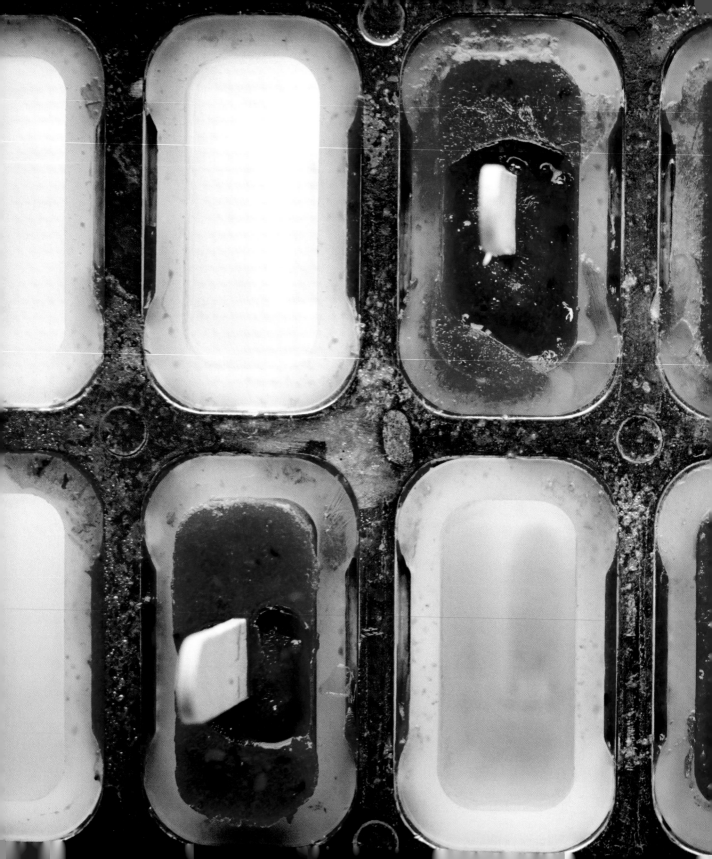

CHAPTER 9

sweet treats and snacks

Once I got rid of the processed sugar

and replaced it with alternative sweeteners, I found I could still make sweet treats everyone would like—but not feel the desire to eat every last morsel. More and more people are using sweeteners like coconut palm sugar and stevia, and I'm hearing that they love the taste without feeling as bloated, erratic, and sugar-crazed. And let's face it: Kids are going to seek out desserts, candy bars, and cookies. Wouldn't you rather give them choices you can feel good about than make them sneak around with candy wrappers in their pockets? Try these out, pick your favorites, and—if your personal eating map allows it—enjoy them without regret.

the recipes

Superfood
SNACK MIX

I'VE BECOME OBSESSED WITH THIS tasty snack, which I feel good about eating in embarrassingly large quantities. In the spirit of making every bite count, each element of this addictive mix earns its nutritional keep. I start with that new superfood darling, dried white mulberries, which taste like caramel and contain less sugar than raisins, dates, and other dried fruit (and that's before you even get to the fiber, antioxidant phenols, and protein). I also throw in vitamin C–laced rose hips; amazing almonds; antioxidant cacao nibs, which add a shot of high-fiber, low-sugar chocolate goodness; and tender, low-carb coconut flakes, which contribute a tropical sweetness and an outsized helping of fiber.

——————Makes 1¾ cups——————

½ cup unsweetened shredded coconut

2 tablespoons cacao nibs (see page 25)

2 tablespoons dried rose hips (see page 28)

½ cup almonds, soaked and dehydrated (see page 32)

½ cup dried white mulberries (see page 26)

In a bowl, combine all of the ingredients. Store in an airtight container for up to 1 month.

Spicy
WALNUTS

THESE NUTS LEND A SWEET, SPICY KICK to snacking. Nosh on them out of hand or use them to add some heat to a tossed green salad. If you like things fiery, add a touch more cayenne to the mix.

—————————*Makes 4 cups*—————————

4 cups walnuts, soaked and dehydrated (see page 32)

½ cup coconut palm sugar (see page 29)

½ teaspoon fine sea salt

¼ teaspoon cayenne pepper

In a large bowl, combine all of the ingredients until incorporated. Pack onto two dehydrator trays lined with nonstick dehydrator sheets (see page 36), allowing the nuts to touch one another. Dehydrate at 115°F until dry, 20 to 24 hours, removing the nuts and flipping them midway through dehydrating. Let cool, then break the nuts into clusters. Store in an airtight container for up to 1 month.

TIP Instead of dehydrating, bake the nuts. Preheat the oven to 175°F or your oven's lowest temperature. Line two baking sheets with parchment paper. Spread the nuts on the sheets and bake, stirring midway through, or until fragrant and lightly golden, 1½ to 2 hours.

My Famous
CANDIED NUTS

A COUNTERTOP STAPLE IN MY HOUSEHOLD, these candied nuts do double duty as a source of nutrition and as a sweet, satisfying treat. If I'm heading to a meeting or a workout and need a power boost, I throw some of these into a cup and snack on them en route. One study demonstrated that people who eat nuts on a regular basis have a longer life span. One thing's for certain: You won't die of hunger if you snack on these. They're fiber-filled, and you'll feel like you've had dessert when, in fact, you've done your body a favor. Use coconut nectar, if you like, because it is lower on the glycemic index, but I stick with maple syrup.

———————*Makes 5 cups*———————

4 cups walnuts or pecans, soaked and dehydrated (see page 32)

1 cup hemp seeds or ¾ cup hemp seeds plus ¼ cup chia seeds

⅓ cup pure maple syrup or coconut nectar (see page 29)

¾ cup unsweetened shredded coconut

1 teaspoon pure vanilla extract

½ teaspoon fine sea salt

In a large bowl, combine all of the ingredients until well incorporated. Pack onto two dehydrator trays lined with nonstick dehydrator sheets (see page 36), allowing the nuts to touch one another. Dehydrate at 118°F until dry, 20 to 24 hours, removing the nuts and flipping them midway through dehydrating, until crisp.

Alternatively, you can bake the nuts: Preheat the oven to 350°F degrees. Line two baking sheets with parchment paper.

Spread the nuts on the sheets and bake, stirring midway through, until fragrant and golden, 15 to 20 minutes.

Let cool, then break the candied nuts into clusters. Store in an airtight container for up to 1 month.

Strawberry
FRUIT LEATHER

PREPARING THE BASE FOR THIS fruit leather is a 5-minute job that reaps rewards which last much longer. Being able to put a homemade, naturally sweet snack into my kids' lunches makes me feel like a superhuman—and I'm the only one who needs to know just how simple the process is. Bonus: Because strawberries are so naturally sweet, a few drops of stevia is all it takes to perfect their flavor.

——Makes four 10-inch rounds——

7 cups strawberries (2½ pounds), hulled and rinsed

1 pear or apple, peeled, cored, and cut into chunks

1 teaspoon fresh lemon juice

3 drops stevia sweetener

In a blender or food processor, puree all of the ingredients until smooth. Pour 2 cups of the puree into the center of a dehydrator tray lined with a nonstick dehydrator sheet (see page 36) and spread into a 10-inch circle, leaving about 1 inch around the border. Repeat with three more lined dehydrator trays and the remaining puree.

Dehydrate the fruit leather at 118°F until the center is firm and dry and the fruit leather peels off easily, 6 to 8 hours.

Peel the leather off the dehydrator sheets and arrange each piece on a sheet of parchment paper. Roll each up into a log and wrap in an additional piece of parchment to keep moist. The fruit leather will keep, tightly wrapped in parchment at room temperature, for up to 3 months.

Fruits for Dehydrating

Some fruits are born to be dehydrated; some aren't. It's all about the delicate balance of fiber, sugar, and liquid in the fruit itself. The best of the bunch are stone fruits like peaches, apricots, nectarines, and plums; pears and apples; and seeded berries like strawberries, blackberries, and raspberries. If you want to dehydrate blueberries, dry them with other berries, not exceeding one third of the entire weight of the fruit.

CRUNCHY MILLET, CARROT, AND TURMERIC MUFFINS

COULD THESE MUFFINS BE FILLED with any more good stuff? From the nutrient-rich almond meal to the hemp seeds, walnuts, dried cherries, and turmeric, they are a veritable market basket of goodness! The tops spread out over the edges and get crispy, and the millet flakes (available in any health food store) add little bits of crunchiness to every morsel. I'm partial to my ceramic muffin tin (see Tip, opposite page), which bakes evenly and encourages crispness and browning, like a pizza stone in muffin-tin form. These muffins freeze beautifully and make great lunchtime desserts for the kids; wrap them individually in parchment paper and include them in school lunches.

—————Makes 6 large or 8 standard muffins—————

Coconut oil cooking spray or baking spray

1½ cups almond meal or almond flour (see Tip, page 260)

¼ cup flax meal

¼ cup hemp seeds

¼ cup millet flakes (see above)

2 tablespoons millet, soaked and dehydrated (see page 32)

½ cup coconut palm sugar (see page 29)

1 teaspoon baking soda

½ teaspoon fine sea salt

½ teaspoon ground cinnamon

¼ teaspoon ground nutmeg

2 large eggs

¼ cup coconut oil (see page 23), melted and slightly cooled

1 teaspoon pure vanilla extract

1 jumbo or 2 medium carrots, peeled and grated

2 teaspoons grated peeled fresh turmeric or ½ teaspoon dried

½ cup dried cherries or dried blueberries, coarsely chopped

½ cup walnuts, soaked and dehydrated (see page 32), chopped

Preheat the oven to 350°F. Spray a 6-compartment jumbo or 8-compartment regular muffin tin with coconut oil cooking spray or baking spray.

In a medium bowl, whisk together the almond meal, flax meal, hemp seeds, millet flakes, millet, coconut palm sugar, baking soda, salt, cinnamon, and nutmeg until incorporated.

In a small bowl, whisk together the eggs, coconut oil, and vanilla. Add the wet ingredients to the dry ingredients and mix until well incorporated. Fold in the carrots, turmeric, dried fruit, and walnuts.

Divide the batter among the compartments in the muffin tin and bake until a tooth-pick inserted into the center of the muffins comes out clean, 30 to 35 minutes. Cool for 5 minutes, then transfer to a baking rack to cool completely. The muffins can be stored in an airtight container for 3 days or frozen for up to 2 months.

TIP You can find ceramic muffin tins online, available on Amazon. My favorite is the Hartstone Pottery six-compartment stoneware muffin tin. If you're making other muffin recipes, these babies hold a lot of batter, so you might want to increase the recipe by half.

RAW CHOCOLATE BARS

FEW KITCHEN ACTIVITIES ARE AS REWARDING as turning out chocolate bars that taste better than virtually anything you'll find in stores, and you'll never buy another one after you've made mine. It's now common knowledge that cacao is a healthy superfood, filled with antioxidant and anti-inflammatory properties, fiber, and other benefits that make me feel extra-good about whipping up these treats from scratch. Starting with the very best ingredients is essential; seek out a block of raw cacao paste (essentially ground-up cacao beans; also known as cacao liquor or chocolate liquor) and raw cocoa butter (solidified pure oil from the cacao bean), products that have been processed at low temperatures to protect their nutritional value. You'll probably have to order one or the other online.

——Makes 8 to 10 (3-inch) bars——

I'm not always the most focused cook—chances are I'm doing three other things while cooking for my family. But when I make chocolate, I go into Zen mode and try to tune out the outside world. More than any other recipe in the book, this one requires your full attention. Chocolate making isn't complicated, but like many pastry and candy projects, it's meticulous work. In this case, an important first step is making sure your grater, mixing bowl, spatula, and whisk are as dry as the Sahara Desert. Even a single drop of water can cause the warm chocolate to "seize," meaning the water grabs onto the dry particles in the mixture, making a grainy mess out of the beautiful raw ingredients.

4 ounces pure cacao paste (see above), available on Amazon

4 ounces pure cocoa butter, available on Amazon

½ cup coconut nectar (see page 29)

1½ teaspoons pure vanilla extract or 1 vanilla bean, split in half and seeds scraped out

⅛ teaspoon fine sea salt

Coconut oil cooking spray

Toppings of your choice (optional)

Dried fruits, such as white mulberries, goji berries, and cherries

Seeds, such as hemp seeds, or sesame seeds, or soaked and dehydrated pepitas (see page 32)

Nuts, such as almonds, walnuts, or hazelnuts, soaked and dehydrated (see page 32)

Using the smaller (but not smallest) holes on a box grater or the larger side of a Microplane grater or a high-speed blender, grate or process the cacao paste (you should have about 2½ cups), then the cocoa butter (you should have 2 cups). Transfer them to a medium bowl (they will look like a black and white snowdrift).

Remove the stacking trays from the dehydrator and set to 115°F. Place the bowl of cacao mixture in the dehydrator and heat until the mixture melts, 30 to 45 minutes (check after 30 minutes and give the chocolate a stir with a silicone spatula).

Remove the bowl from the dehydrator, add the coconut nectar, vanilla extract or seeds, and salt, whisk to combine, then return to the dehydrator for 5 minutes.

Remove the mixture from the dehydrator and transfer to a flexible silicone measuring cup or a candy-making funnel. Spray the desired molds (see Tips below) with coconut oil spray, place on a baking sheet, and carefully fill the molds with the chocolate. Sprinkle with the toppings of your choice, if desired. Refrigerate until solid, 10 to 15 minutes.

Pop the chocolates out of the molds and marvel at how incredibly amazing they look and taste! The chocolates can be refrigerated, wrapped individually in parchment paper, for up to 1 month.

TIPS Cacao paste and cocoa butter can be purchased from Navitasnaturals.com.

Use any molds you want, from 3-ounce chocolate-bar ones to minis that produce tiny individual candies. You'll find a good selection of molds on Amazon, Wilton.com, and Etsy.

Power-Packed
DATE AND TAHINI TRUFFLES

CAN YOU SAY YUM? By choosing naturally sweet ingredients, you get a decadent confection with a low glycemic load. Both the tahini and the mesquite powder are good sources of protein, making them a great pre- or post-gym pick-me-up. In this recipe, the mesquite also serves to absorb the tahini's natural oils, helping create the perfect texture and taste.

Makes 12 truffles

6 ounces (about 14) Medjool dates, pitted

2½ tablespoons raw tahini, store-bought or homemade (page 95)

3 tablespoons mesquite powder (see page 27)

½ teaspoon ashwagandha (see page 25)

⅛ teaspoon fine sea salt

In a food processor, process the dates until finely chopped (or finely chop by hand). Add the tahini, mesquite powder, ashwagandha, and salt, and process until incorporated; the mixture will look like large grains of sand. Alternatively, put the ingredients in a bowl and mix with a wooden spoon until incorporated.

Using damp hands, press the mixture into a cohesive dough and roll into 12 balls. Chill slightly, if desired, before serving. Store in a single layer in an airtight container for up to 2 weeks.

Coco Loco
MACAROONS

THIS IS WHAT THE DEHYDRATOR was invented for. It purrs in the corner, so quiet you might not realize it's busy transforming delish ingredients into these irresistible raw kisses. I'm a real lover of coconut, not the least because it's great for making hair and skin shiny. It's also a good source of fiber and extremely low in carbs, so it helps keep your blood sugar levels in check. Coconut has also been found to lower cholesterol. The chia seeds look like poppy seeds and add protein, fiber, and omega-3s. Make sure you use unsweetened shredded coconut, not the candied stuff in the baking aisle at the supermarket.

——————*Makes 20 macaroons*——————

2 cups unsweetened shredded coconut

½ cup almond flour or
almond meal (see Tip)

¼ cup solid coconut oil (see page 23)

¼ cup coconut nectar (see page 29)

2 tablespoons chia seeds

2 tablespoons cacao nibs
(see page 25; optional)

1 vanilla bean, split in half
and seeds scraped out, or 1
teaspoon pure vanilla extract

¼ teaspoon fine sea salt

With a hand mixer in a large bowl or in a stand mixer fitted with the paddle attachment, beat all the ingredients until the mixture holds together when pinched. Using your hands, make free-form macaroons using 1½ tablespoons dough for each.

Arrange the macaroons 2 inches apart on dehydrator trays lined with nonstick dehydrator sheets (see page 36). Dehydrate at 118°F, flipping halfway through, until dried on the exterior but still moist on the inside, about 12 hours. The macaroons can be stored in an airtight container for up to 2 weeks.

TIP Instead of dehydrating, you can bake the macaroons on a parchment-lined baking sheet at 350°F for about 15 minutes, or until lightly golden.

Almond Meal and Almond Flour

Though almond meal (coarsely ground unblanched almonds) and almond flour (ground blanched almonds) can be purchased at most health food stores, you can also make your own. Place soaked, dehydrated almonds (see page 32) in a high-speed blender and pulse, stopping to scrape down the sides, until very fine. Make sure you don't overprocess, which overheats the nuts and releases valuable oils.

shari's rules *for* cheating-eating

1. Treat yourself! We can't live on celery sticks alone.

2. If you like sweets, eat them. Find ways to sub in healthier alternatives, and exercise portion control: Don't eat the whole pan. The recipes in this book offer solutions so that the sweet tooth is satisfied and the body remains healthy.

3. Let your kids indulge when they are out and about. Forbidding everything only makes them want it more.

4. At home, offer great choices and let your kids be in charge of the dessert. If there is no refined sugar around, they will use alternatives!

5. Get back on the wagon as soon as you fall off. An occasional digression from the usual plan won't derail you.

6. Let it go!

Nut-Butter
LACE COOKIES

WATCHING THE BATTER FOR THESE COOKIES transform into lacy rounds is pure culinary magic. The cookies contain protein, thanks to the nut butter and/or eggs (see Tip), plus the added health benefits of flax meal, apple, and ashwagandha. Since moisture is the enemy of crispness, make sure you cool these cookies completely before storing them in an airtight container.

—————*Makes 24 cookies*—————

1¾ cups coconut palm sugar (see page 29)

1¾ cups unsweetened shredded coconut

½ cup Chicory sweetener (see page 30)

½ cup almond or coconut milk

¼ cup melted coconut oil (see page 23)

¼ cup flax meal

¼ teaspoon fine sea salt (if using unsalted nut butter)

1 vanilla bean, split in half and seeds scraped out, or 1½ teaspoons pure vanilla extract

½ cup finely chopped unpeeled apple

2 teaspoons ashwagandha (see page 25)

¾ cup hazelnut, almond, or sunflower seed butter, store-bought or homemade (page 97)

Preheat the oven to 375°F. Line two baking sheets with parchment paper.

With a hand mixer in a large bowl or in a stand mixer fitted with the paddle attachment, combine all of the ingredients and beat on medium speed until smooth, about 1 minute. Drop the batter by the tablespoonful onto the baking sheets, leaving 4 inches of space between them.

Bake until the cookies spread and the edges are crisped, rotating the sheets from top to bottom and front to back halfway through the baking, 16 to 18 minutes total. Transfer the cookies, still on the parchment paper, to racks and let cool completely. Peel the cookies off the parchment. The cookies can be stored in an airtight container for up to 2 weeks.

TIP For cakier, non-vegan cookies, substitute 2 large eggs for the almond or coconut milk.

CHOCOLATE CHIP AND HEMP SEED COOKIES

YOU ONLY LIVE ONCE, and preferably, chocolate chips are involved—often. That's why I make these cookies. Between the hemp seeds, the almond flour, and the antioxidant-rich chocolate chips, these are cookies that don't require confession after eating. They keep for a good 5 days if stored in an airtight container and also freeze well; if you warm them in the oven, do so for 10 minutes at 200°F. The chocolate gets all gooey, and the heat brings out the toastiness of the coconut. Sweeeeet!

——————Makes 40 cookies ——————

2½ cups almond flour or almond meal (see Tip, page 260)

¼ cup hemp seeds

½ cup coconut flour (see page 26)

½ cup unsweetened shredded coconut

½ teaspoon fine sea salt

1 teaspoon baking soda

2 large eggs

½ cup coconut palm sugar (see page 29) or pure maple syrup

1 teaspoon pure vanilla extract

½ cup coconut oil (see page 23), solid or melted

1 (12-ounce) bag dairy-free semisweet chocolate chips, mini or regular

Preheat the oven to 375°F. Line two baking sheets with parchment paper.

In a medium bowl, combine the almond flour, hemp seeds, coconut flour, shredded coconut, salt, and baking soda. In another bowl, beat the eggs, coconut palm sugar, and vanilla extract with a hand mixer or wooden spoon until incorporated. Gradually add the wet ingredients to the dry and beat until well combined. Beat in the coconut oil until incorporated, then fold in the chocolate chips.

Scoop walnut-sized balls of dough onto the baking sheets, leaving 2 inches between them. Bake until the tops are slightly golden, rotating the sheets halfway through baking, 9 to 11 minutes total. Cool on racks. The cookies can be stored in an airtight container for up to 5 days at room temperature or up to 1 month in the freezer.

TIP If you prefer your cookies flatter, use the maple syrup and melted coconut oil; for firmer, thicker cookies, use the coconut palm sugar and leave the coconut oil in its natural solid form.

Nutty Goji-Millet
CRISPY TREATS

I LOVED RICE KRISPIES TREATS AS A KID, but I didn't know that with every bite, I was eating a sugar rocket that sent my blood glucose into the stratosphere. A series of healthy swap-ins make these an easily grabbable snack when you're looking for a sweet energy booster. Medjool dates—the really fudgy, sticky, plump ones usually grown in the Middle East or California—take the place of the sugary marshmallow. The dates have a drastically lower glycemic profile than white sugar, not to mention healthy fiber and potassium. I also love the way the hemp seeds and goji berries add color and pack in tons of additional superfood power. And—oh, yeah—my kids *and* my mom love them.

————Makes 16 squares————

Coconut oil cooking spray
or baking spray

1 cup chopped pitted Medjool dates

1 cup almond or sunflower seed butter,
store-bought or homemade (page 97)

3 tablespoons coconut nectar (see
page 29), plus more if necessary

1 tablespoon psyllium husks (see
page 28), dissolved in ¼ cup
warm water for 10 minutes

½ teaspoon fine sea salt

3½ cups puffed millet cereal

¼ cup hemp seeds

¼ cup dried goji berries

Spray an 8-inch square baking dish with coconut oil cooking spray or baking spray.

In a stand mixer fitted with the paddle attachment, beat the dates on medium-high speed until smooth and the date paste coats the sides of the bowl, about 30 seconds. Scrape down the sides of the bowl. Add the almond butter, coconut nectar, dissolved psyllium husks, and salt and beat on medium-high speed until the dates and nut butter are incorporated and creamy, about 30 seconds. Reduce the speed to low, add the millet cereal, hemp seeds, and goji berries, and mix until just combined, 5 to 10 seconds.

Press some of the mixture between your hands; if it sticks together easily, great. If not, add another tablespoon of coconut nectar and try again.

Press the mixture into the baking dish, pressing down firmly to help it stick together. Refrigerate for 1 hour to firm, then cut into 16 squares and serve. The treats can be stored in an airtight container for up to 5 days.

Apple and Pear
CRUMBLE

USE ANY COMBINATION OF APPLES and pears you like, then top with our granola bars in any flavor your heart desires—a premade topping just waiting to crown a dish of spiced fruit and other goodies. In addition to helping absorb the fruit's natural juices, the coconut flour adds great texture and taste in combination with cinnamon and nutmeg. Don't peel the fruit. Over half the fiber in an apple comes from the skin, so leave it intact. I'm partial to our Cranberry Granola bars here—the way the tart dried fruit contrasts with the sweet apples is dessert heaven.

————————*Serves 6 to 8*————————

Coconut oil cooking spray
or baking spray

4 large unpeeled apples,
cored and chopped

3 ripe, firm, unpeeled pears,
cored and chopped

¼ cup dried yacon slices (see page 28)

2 tablespoons coconut
flour (see page 26)

3 tablespoons coconut palm
sugar (see page 29)

½ teaspoon ground cinnamon

¼ teaspoon ground nutmeg

4 Two Moms in the Raw Granola bars,
preferably Cranberry, crumbled

2 tablespoons coconut oil
(see page 23), melted

⅛ teaspoon flaky sea salt

Sweet Coconut Cream (page
272), for serving

Preheat the oven to 375°F. Spray a 9-by-13-inch baking dish with coconut oil spray or baking spray and set aside.

In a large bowl, toss together the apples, pears, yacon, coconut flour, coconut palm sugar, cinnamon, and nutmeg. Transfer the mixture to the baking dish and bake until the fruit releases some of its liquid, 15 to 20 minutes.

Meanwhile, in a medium bowl, toss the crumbled granola bars with the oil and salt. Sprinkle the granola mixture over the top of the fruit.

Reduce the oven temperature to 350°F and bake until the apples are softened and the granola is fragrant and golden, 15 to 20 minutes. Serve warm or at room temperature, topped with Sweet Coconut Cream.

RAW KEY LIME PIE

IF THERE'S ONE DESSERT I'M KNOWN FOR, it's this raw pie, which I make for every special occasion (and many not-so-special ones, too). More than one person has suggested I sell it, but instead, I'm giving the recipe to you. The crust starts with soaked, dehydrated nuts, which I blend with coconut and bind with rich, sticky Medjool dates before pressing into a springform pan. (If I have candied nuts on hand, I blend those up instead of the pecans for the crust.) For the filling, I make an occasional cheater's exception to my no-cashew rule, because nothing beats the creamy texture they achieve (macadamia nuts will ably sub in, though). Do not dehydrate the cashews, or they won't be creamy. Since this is supposed to be sweet and tart, ½ cup sweetener goes a long way. You might be tempted to use bottled Key lime juice— never! Squeezing the Key limes is worthwhile work, but if you can't find the tiny green fruits, use regular limes.

————————Serves 8————————

For the crust

2 cups pecans, soaked and dehydrated (see page 32)

3 heaping tablespoons hemp seeds

1 cup unsweetened shredded coconut

¼ teaspoon fine sea salt

¼ cup pitted Medjool dates

For the filling

1½ cups cashews, soaked for 20 to 30 minutes, rinsed, and drained (do not dehydrate)

Finely grated zest of 2 Key limes or ½ regular lime

6 tablespoons fresh Key (or regular) lime juice

6 tablespoons coconut oil (see page 23)

¼ cup raw agave nectar or coconut nectar (see page 29)

¼ cup water

1 vanilla bean, split in half and seeds scraped out

¼ teaspoon fine sea salt

For serving

1 lime, very thinly sliced

Fresh lime juice

Sweet Coconut Cream (recipe follows; optional)

Make the crust: In a bowl, toss the pecans, hemp seeds, shredded coconut, and salt. Spread on two dehydrator trays lined with nonstick dehydrator sheets (see page 36) and dehydrate at 118°F for 24 hours, flipping halfway through. (Or bake on a parchment-paper-lined baking sheet at 350°F until fragrant and lightly golden, 15 to 20 minutes.) Let cool.

Sweet Treats and Snacks

Break the mixture apart, transfer to a blender or food processor, add the dates, and pulse until the mixture is sticky and holds together when pinched. Press into a 9-inch springform pan, pressing the crust across the bottom and up the sides of the pan.

Make the filling: Combine all of the ingredients in a blender and process until smooth, 30 to 45 seconds. Pour into the pie shell and freeze until solid, at least 8 hours or up to 24. Garnish with lime slices and a squeeze of lime juice. If desired, serve with a dollop of Sweet Coconut Cream.

—————

SWEET COCONUT CREAM

GETTING MY FAMILY TO SOFT-PEDAL it on the dairy is a lot easier when replacements like this exist. Chilling the coconut milk (sorry, light just won't do here) allows the cream to literally rise to the top. Whipping it into a fluffy cloud is a snap, and it holds its shape in the fridge for a full day. You're going to want to make this dessert staple a lot, so keep a couple of cans of coconut milk in the fridge at all times. I like to serve this with fresh fruit, Raw Key Lime Pie (page 271), and Apple and Pear Crumble (page 268).

————Serves 4 to 6————

1 (13.5-ounce) can coconut milk (not light)

⅓ cup coconut palm sugar (see page 29)

2 tablespoons arrowroot powder

½ teaspoon pure vanilla extract

¼ teaspoon fine sea salt

Chill the unopened can of coconut milk in the refrigerator for at least 4 hours. Invert the can, open it, and drain off the liquid, reserving it for another use.

Place the solidified coconut cream in a stand mixer fitted with the whisk attachment and beat on high speed until thick, 1 to 2 minutes. Alternatively, you can use a hand mixer and a large bowl. Add the remaining ingredients and whip for 1 minute. The topping can be made in advance and refrigerated, covered with plastic wrap, for up to 24 hours.

Frozen
LUCUMA-COCONUT MOUSSE

THIS CREAMY, DREAMY DESSERT WILL make you forget dairy-based ice creams once and for all. Making it requires a little advance planning, since you have to chill the coconut milk first, but trust me, it's worth it. The rich, smooth coconut cream melds with the natural sweetness of lucuma, a South American superfood packed with antioxidants and fiber, allowing you to use far less sweetener than you would in ordinary ice cream. For kicks, I've suggested all kinds of mix-ins; let your whims dictate what you choose to throw in. Though I've found the blender method yields a fluffier, airier, and less icy dessert, you can also process the mixture in a traditional ice cream maker following the manufacturer's instructions.

—Serves 4 to 6—

4 (13.5-ounce) cans coconut milk (not light)

6 tablespoons lucuma powder (see page 27)

10 Medjool dates, pitted

2 vanilla beans, split in half and seeds scraped out, or 1 tablespoon pure vanilla extract

¼ teaspoon fine sea salt

Mix-ins (optional)

2 tablespoons cacao nibs (see page 25)

½ cup unsweetened shredded coconut

¼ cup chopped pitted Medjool dates

¼ cup chopped bittersweet chocolate

Chill the unopened cans of coconut milk in the refrigerator for at least 4 hours and up to 24, until the cans feel solid. Invert the cans, open, drain off the liquid and reserve.

Transfer the solidified coconut cream to a blender and add the lucuma, dates, vanilla seeds or extract, and salt. Blend until smooth and creamy, 15 to 30 seconds, scraping down the sides of the blender if necessary.

Divide the ice cream base among two ice cube trays and freeze until solid, at least 4 hours.

Transfer the cubes to a blender or food processor and pulse, adding the reserved liquid as needed until the desired consistency is achieved. Gently fold in the desired mix-ins and serve immediately.

For a frozen mousse, return to the freezer for 1 hour before serving.

Owen's
"BARRY" POPS

THESE FROZEN POPS TAKE JUST a few minutes to make and work with any ripe, luscious fruit. I named this recipe for the way my son, Owen, spelled "strawberry" when he helped me develop the recipe. I'm a fan of the prefrozen pop molds made by Zoku; keep them in the freezer, and they're ready to make fully formed ice pops in 7 to 9 minutes! I've suggested several mix-ins to further boost the pops' nutritional benefits.

——————Makes 4 pops——————

2½ cups fresh fruit, such as chopped strawberries, mango, pineapple, or kiwis, or whole blueberries, blackberries, or raspberries

2 tablespoons fresh lemon or lime juice

2 tablespoons coconut nectar or palm sugar (see page 29)

Mix-ins (optional)

1 tablespoon dried yacon slices (see page 28)

1 (100-gram) unsweetened frozen açai smoothie pack (see page 25)

2 teaspoons maqui powder (see page 27)

In a blender, puree all of the ingredients, including any desired mix-ins, until smooth. Pour into freezer pop molds and freeze until solid.

RESOURCES

Books

These books helped guide me in my journey to healing and recovery.

Boroch, Ann. *Healing Multiple Sclerosis: Diet, Detox & Nutritional Makeover for Total Recovery.* Quintessential Healing, 2013.

Cousens, Gabriel, MD. *Rainbow Green Live-Food Cuisine.* North Atlantic Books, 2003.

Mars, Brigitte. *Rawsome! Maximizing Health, Energy, and Culinary Delight with the Raw Foods Diet.* Basic Health Publications, 2004.

Wahls, Terry L., MD. *Minding My Mitochondria: How I Overcame Secondary Progressive Multiple Sclerosis (MS) and Got Out of My Wheelchair.* 2nd edition, TZ Press, 2010; *The Wahls Protocol: How I Beat Progressive MS Using Paleo Principles and Functional Medicine,* Avery, 2014.

Products

For Two Moms in the Raw products, go to our web site, Twomomsintheraw.com.

Navitasnaturals.com offers a good variety of the powders and dried fruits called for in this book, including açai, cacao paste, chia seeds, goji berries, white mulberries, maqui, and yacon.

Edenfoods.com stocks nori sheets (seaweed), brown rice noodles, and gomasio.

Whole Foods Market is a great source for bulk organic raw nuts and seeds, as well as canned goods like coconut milk, organic tomatoes, and coconut water.

INDEX

(Page references in *italics* refer to illustrations.)